MICHIGAN ICE HOCKEY

MICHIGAN ICE HOCKEY

Celebrating the All-Time Greats and Most Memorable Moments

GREG NELSON

Ann Arbor
University of Michigan Press

Published in the United States of America by
The University of Michigan Press
Manufactured in the United States of America

∞ Printed on acid-free paper

ISBN-13: 978-0-472-03444-4

2013 2012 2011 2010 4 3 2 1

Cover photo by Adam Jacobs
Use of Block M granted by the University of Michigan Trademark Licensing Office.

Dedication

Thanks to Lori, Erik, Marisa, Drew, Jacob, and Analise, as well as the many supportive friends and relatives who offered their love and encouragement. God bless you all.

Additional thanks to Kelly Sippell for her dedication and enthusiasm and to the entire University of Michigan hockey family—the players, coaches, and fans who set the program apart from all the others.

Contents

Home Ice Advantage 1

Champions of the West—and Beyond 17

Players and Coaches 39

Shots on Goal 61

The Record Book—Team Records/Awards 87

The Record Book—Individual Records/Awards 111

Home Ice Advantage

While the 1911 UM hockey squad skated outdoors on the frozen Huron River, today's teams vie for national championships in state-of-the-art arenas.

Frozen Rivers to Frozen Fours

Many National Hockey League stars look back on their childhood days and reminisce about playing on frozen lakes and backyard rinks. Today, the University of Michigan's illustrious ice hockey program can hark back to its own infancy in much the same way.

All it takes is one winter's evening in Ann Arbor to see how far the Wolverines have come from the days of skating outdoors on the city's frozen Huron River to playing before large and zany crowds at venerable Yost Arena and grandiose rinks nationwide.

This is the story of a fan base with a passion for pucks and a love for its conquering heroes on skates. This is an intimate look at the people, the traditions, the lore, and the statistics associated with a program that has won more collegiate hockey titles than any other university in America.

From its humble beginnings to its current status as one of the nation's elite programs, nothing sums up the joys of collegiate hockey like Go Blue!

Ice Chips

Yesterday and Today

While hockey at the University of Michigan began along the banks of the frozen Huron River, the sport's first organized indoor game was played in Canada on March 3, 1875, at the Victoria Skating Rink in Montreal. The game, arranged by James Creighton, featured two nine-player teams that included Creighton and a number of students from McGill University. The teams utilized a puck, goal posts set 6 feet apart (still the standard size today), and the game lasted 60 minutes, another constant for regulation time in today's game. Two years later, in 1877, the first ice hockey club was formed, called the McGill University Hockey Club. Many of the rules of today's game were also set forth at that time by Creighton and his colleagues, using field hockey as their guide.

With fast and furious action and a raucous home crowd, Michigan ice hockey remains one of the most vibrant and popular sports on campus.

Experience Michigan Hockey

Collegiate ice hockey is one of the fastest, most entertaining sports on earth. Want proof? Just step inside the University of Michigan's historic Yost Arena and witness fast-paced end-to-end skating, heart-pounding body checks, and frozen rubber pucks being shot at nearly 100 miles per hour. Yet in Ann Arbor, the action is not just confined to the ice. Game in and game out, the loud and boisterous Wolverines fans truly become a part of the action long before the first puck ever drops. Students hold up newspapers and chant "Who Cares?" while the opposing team is being introduced. Through its creative chants and amusing interaction with the Michigan Ice Hockey Pep Band, the vocal home crowd helps create the best, most imposing home ice atmosphere anywhere in the game.

The pep band ensures that Yost Arena rocks throughout each game, offering everything from spirited renditions of *Hail to the Victors* to leading the creative home crowd in fun-filled verbal mocking of the opposition. In fact, the pep band and Michigan hockey fanatics are always in tune with what is happening on the ice and always ready to provide comedic and innovative interaction. You simply never know what might happen next.

Ice Chips

Intimidation Factor

Yost Arena's intimidation factor has long resulted in exemplary records in front of the Wolverine's loud and loyal fan base. The intimidation was never more visible than a six-year stretch from 1991–92 until 1996–97 when Michigan's ice hockey teams compiled a home record of 94-7-8, while never losing more than two games in front of the Yost faithful. That win total also included one undefeated home season when UM ran off an 18-0-2 home record in 1996–97.

After more than a decade of trying to get their sport recognized by the university, the Huron Hockey Club finally gained varsity status at UM in 1922.

The Most Humble of Beginnings

Michigan's storied hockey history began with the most humble of beginnings—on the frozen ice of the Huron River, which runs through the city of Ann Arbor. Using the most rudimentary forms of equipment, the young men of the Huron Hockey Club began to generate some interest in the game during the early 1900s. The group petitioned the University of Michigan to gain varsity status in 1911, only to be denied. Undaunted, the group moved forward, and by 1916 interest in ice skating was growing across the campus and becoming more and more popular among students. It wasn't until December 1922, however, that the club finally became an official Michigan varsity sport.

Ice Chips

Their First Home

Far removed from the cozy amenities of today's ice hockey rinks, the Wolverines played their first season in the Weinberg Coliseum. The simple structure featured concrete walls and was open on one end. As a result, any attempts to play hockey were fully dependent on the cooperation of the weather and temperatures staying cold enough to keep the ice surface frozen. While Fielding H. Yost was busy christening a new field house and building other athletic structures on the Michigan campus, he purchased the Coliseum in 1925. Having previously added spectator stands and boards in 1923 plus an additional 30 feet of ice in 1927 to create a full-size rink, Yost eventually constructed a fourth wall to the Coliseum in 1928, and the building went on to serve as the permanent home of Michigan ice hockey for 50 years.

Yost Arena remains the toughest rink for opponents in America, and the Wolverines feed off the energy of the maize and blue faithful within the building.

America's Toughest Rink

Home ice. Few hockey rinks provide a home ice advantage quite like venerable Yost Arena. With its passionate, energized, and creative crowds, Yost has long been considered one of the nation's toughest rinks for opponents to play. In 2004, an informal poll conducted by *American Hockey Magazine* listed Yost Arena as the nation's toughest rink for opponents. In April 1997, a *Sports Illustrated* article also chronicled the Arena's crowd-crazy atmosphere. Spurred on by a variety of ingenious taunts and cheers, the University of Michigan crowd is nothing short of relentless with its noise and verbal assaults on the opposing teams, players, and fans while motivating the maize and blue home team to reach for their maximum effort. When UM scores a goal, students quickly remind the opposing goalie how many goals he has allowed, let him know they want more, and tell him he's a sieve and that it's all his fault. It's all in a night's work for the home fans!

Ice Chips

Streaking . . . 33-0-3

Michigan's amazing home ice advantage reached its peak in the 1990s when the Wolverines reeled off a record 36-game home unbeaten streak. It began with a victory on November 11, 1995, and over the course of the next three seasons, Michigan compiled an impressive home ice record of 33-0-3 until Colgate University ended the undefeated streak by knocking off UM on October 17, 1997.

Michigan's longest winning streak on home ice reached 17 on two separate occasions, each over the span of two seasons. The first win streak ran 17 games from March 3, 1961, thru March 3, 1962. And a similar streak ran from January 15, 1993, thru January 21, 1994. In addition to the record 36-game unbeaten (wins and ties) streak, the Wolverines also had home-unbeaten streaks of 19 games (18-0-1 from February 16, 1948, thru December 17, 1949) and 18 games (17-0-1 from February 8, 1956, thru December 6, 1957).

Ever the innovator, Fielding H. Yost was the mastermind behind much of UM's extraordinary athletic campus, including Yost Arena.

The Old Barn

Built in 1923 as a traditional field house and aptly named after Michigan's legendary football coach and athletic director Fielding H. Yost, the building was converted into an ice arena in 1973. Since then, the "Old Barn" has become one of the true hockey shrines in the United States.

Having been renovated in 1996 and again in 2001, the intimate and charming Yost Arena offers a unique historical ambience and an up-close feel for more than 6,600 fans while providing the very best in modern-day locker rooms and facilities for the players. All in all, Yost Arena remains one of the most vocal and raucous hockey venues anywhere and is a favorite place to play for both the Wolverines and their opponents.

Ice Chips

First of its Kind

Upon its completion in 1923, Yost became the nation's first field house. The building quickly became home to a variety of Michigan sports teams, including track and basketball, while also serving as a practice facility for the football and baseball programs. The field house was officially converted into Yost Ice Arena in 1973 and the Wolverines dedicated the new facility by hosting and defeating Waterloo Lutheran 6-2 in the Arena's first hockey game on November 2, 1973. Additional Arena renovations took place in 1992, 1996, 2001, and 2006.

Michigan and in-state rival Michigan State University took the game outside in 2001, attracting a then-record crowd to Spartan Stadium.

Taking It Outside

The Wolverines' storied history began on the outdoor ice of Ann Arbor, but on October 6, 2001, Michigan and Michigan State University gave an entirely new meaning to outdoor hockey. The Spartans and Wolverines attracted a world record hockey crowd of 74,544 plus an international television audience for a game played on a rink set up in the middle of MSU's Spartan Stadium in East Lansing, Michigan. The teams skated to a dramatic 3-3 tie in the "Cold War" and in the process, kick-started a trend of additional outdoor college and NHL games. Michigan skated on the outside ice for a second time on February 6, 2010, in Wisconsin's Camp Randall Stadium, dropping a 3-2 decision to the Badgers in front of 55,031 fans. The game time temperature in Madison, Wisconsin, was in the low twenties, with wind chills falling to as low as 10 degrees.

Ice Chips

Big Chill in the Big House

A Michigan vs. Michigan State outdoor rematch will be held on December 11, 2010. "The Big Chill in the Big House" game is certain to set a new world attendance record for ice hockey when the teams take to the ice in the Wolverines' famed football stadium. The rink will be placed in the center of the stadium with the center ice red line running on top of the 50-yard line. It will be the fifth outdoor game in Division 1 men's ice hockey and the third involving UM.

Date	Teams/Result	Venue	Attendance
10/6/2001	Michigan 3 Michigan State 3	Spartan Stadium	74,544
2/11/2006	Wisconsin 4 Ohio State 2	Lambeau Field	40,890
1/1/2009	Boston Univ. 3 Boston College 2	Fenway Park	38,472
1/8/2009	Wisconsin 3 Michigan 2	Camp Randall	55,031

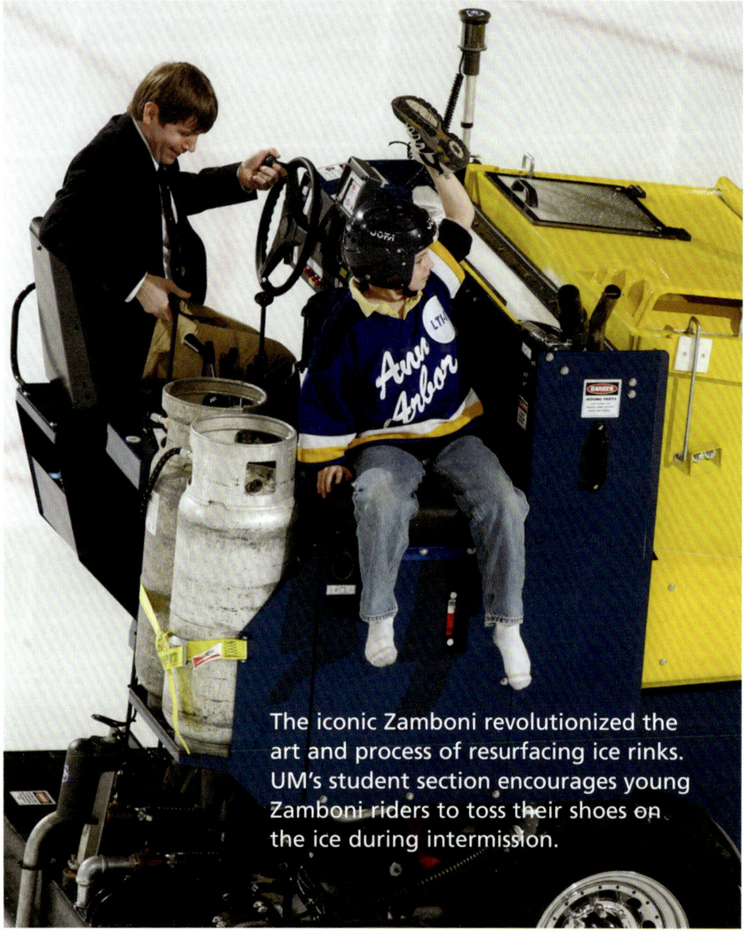

The iconic Zamboni revolutionized the art and process of resurfacing ice rinks. UM's student section encourages young Zamboni riders to toss their shoes on the ice during intermission.

Who Wants to Drive?

While Michigan's earliest teams often played on soft ice filled with shavings, today's game enjoys the benefits of modern technology designed to keep the ice surface at ideal conditions. At Yost Arena, the concrete floor contains three miles of refrigerant piping. Hockey lines and faceoff circles are drawn on the white concrete floor before the area is flooded to form a sheet of ice slightly less than 1.25 inches thick. The Arena utilizes two Zamboni ice-resurfacing machines that can put down a clean, fresh sheet of ice within six minutes. During intermission of Michigan games, the Zamboni often carries an extra passenger in a special seat where children can enjoy the ride of their life. This also offers the Yost Arena crowd with another opportunity to maintain its energy as they encourage Zamboni riders to wave or even take off their shoes and throw them on the ice.

Ice Chips

Ice Cleaning

Every hockey fan is familiar with the appearance of the funny-looking ice-resurfacing machine developed and made famous by Frank J. Zamboni. It took seven years of experimenting before he was able to successfully create a machine that would shave the ice, remove the shavings, wash and squeegee the ice, and hold snow in an elevated tank large enough to last long enough to resurface all of the ice. But by 1949, Zamboni applied for a patent for his "Model A Zamboni Ice Resurfacer," and in 1953 Patent Application No. 93,478 was granted by the U.S. Patent and Trademark Office. While the Zamboni has undergone a number of updates since then, the odd-looking contraption remains one of the most recognizable sights at any hockey game from Ann Arbor to Europe.

Champions of the West—and Beyond

Michigan, Michigan State, Notre Dame, and Michigan Tech all joined the CCHA together in time for the start of the 1981–82 season.

A League of Its Own

While other University of Michigan teams continue to battle for championships in the Big Ten Conference, the Wolverine ice hockey team continues to make its mark in a league of its own—the Central Collegiate Hockey Association (CCHA).

In addition to the Wolverines, other current CCHA member institutions include Alaska–Fairbanks (Nanooks), Bowling Green (Falcons), Ferris State (Bulldogs), Lake Superior State (Lakers), Miami (OH) (Redhawks), Michigan State (Spartans), Nebraska at Omaha (Mavericks), Northern Michigan (Wildcats), Notre Dame (Fighting Irish), Ohio State (Buckeyes), and Western Michigan (Broncos).

Ice Chips

Switching Leagues

Prior to joining the CCHA, the Wolverines played in both the Big Ten and the Western Collegiate Hockey Association (WCHA). Michigan, Michigan State, Notre Dame, and Michigan Tech all entered the CCHA at the start of the 1981–82 season. Those four teams also faced off in the 1981 Great Lakes Invitational (GLI) tournament, the first time the GLI included four teams from the same conference. Michigan won Big Ten hockey titles in 1961, 1962, 1964, 1968, and 1969 and also claimed the WCHA championship in 1964.

Since their first meeting on January 23, 1923, Michigan and the University of Minnesota have remained fierce and storied rivals, facing off annually in the College Hockey Showcase.

87 Years and Counting

Michigan. Minnesota. Michigan State. Wisconsin. They represent four of the most storied and successful programs in collegiate hockey history, combining for a total of 21 NCAA championships. Big Ten Conference rivals in other sports, their hockey allegiances were split in 1981 when Michigan and MSU left the WCHA for the CCHA. The annual College Hockey Showcase was created in 1993 to maintain these decades-old rivalries.

One of the most memorable goals in Michigan history happened against Minnesota on March 24, 1996, in a NCAA West Regional game. Trailing by a goal, Wolverine Mike Legg skated behind the net, flipped the puck onto his stick, and in an instant flicked it lacrosse-style past the stunned goaltender. The extraordinary goal quickly became the stuff of legends, capturing worldwide attention—not to mention an ESPN channel ESPY Award winner for "Outrageous Play of the Year." The Wolverines went on to win the game and six days later captured their eighth national championship!

To see video of the coolest goal ever scored, visit: http://sports.espn.go.com/espn/page2/story?page=hruby/100408_mike_legg_michigan_goal.

Ice Chips

Michigan Rivals

Michigan State University—National Champions: 1966, 1986, 2007
First game vs. Michigan: 1/24/25 Michigan 6, MSU 3

University of Minnesota—National Champions: 1974, 1976, 1979, 2002, 2003
First game vs. Michigan: 1/23/23 Minnesota 2, Michigan 0

University of Wisconsin—National Champions: 1973, 1977, 1981, 1983, 1990, 2006
First game vs. Michigan: 1/12/23 Michigan 2, Wisconsin 1 (2 OT)*

*Michigan's first official varsity game

Since joining the league in 1981–82, UM teams have been sitting atop of the CCHA, racking up nine CCHA tournament championships and 10 CCHA regular season titles.

Champions of the West . . . and the CCHA

Since joining the Central Collegiate Hockey Association (CCHA) for the start of the 1981–82 season, Michigan has racked up 10 regular season conference championships while also claiming the Mason Cup as CCHA Tournament champions nine times. In 2004–05, the Wolverines (23-3-2) set CCHA records for wins, points (48), and winning percentage (.857) in a 28-game conference schedule.

Ice Chips

Michigan in the CCHA

CCHA tournament champions:
1994, 1996, 1997, 1999, 2002, 2003, 2005, 2008, 2010

CCHA regular season champions:
1992, 1994, 1995, 1996, 1997, 2000, 2002, 2004, 2005, 2008

Michigan, celebrating its 1996 title, is co-host of the annual Great Lakes Invitational tournament, one of college hockey's most prestigious events.

By Invitation Only

The Great Lakes Invitational Collegiate Hockey Tournament was created in 1965 as a way to develop more American-born players while improving both the overall quality of play and the popularity of the college game. The tournament is still going strong.

Today, the holiday tournament held annually at Joe Louis Arena in Detroit is one of college hockey's most exciting and most anticipated events of the season. The Wolverines joined Michigan Tech as tournament co-host in 1974, and Michigan State joined as an annual member of the four-team field in 1979. A fourth team is invited to join the action each year. To date, the tournament has included 29 different teams and hosted more than one million fans.

Ice Chips

Lucky 13

Since the tournament's inception, the Wolverines have captured a record 13 Great Lakes Invitational titles: 1966, 1975, 1988, 1989, 1990, 1991, 1992, 1993, 1994, 1995, 1996, 2007, 2008.

Year	Opponent	Result
1966	Michigan Tech	W 4-3
	Michigan State	W 5-3
1968	Michigan Tech	L 2-3
	Michigan State	L 2-4
1970	Brown	W 4-1
	Michigan Tech	L 2-7
1972	Harvard	L 4-8
	Boston University	W 3-7
1974	Harvard	W 3-2
	Michigan Tech	L 2-3
1975	Pennsylvania	W 7-6
	Michigan Tech	W 6-5
1976	Brown	W 7-2
	Michigan Tech	L 6-7
1977	Lake Superior State	W 4-3 OT
	Michigan Tech	L 3-8

Year	Opponent	Result
1978	Ohio State	L 4-5
	Boston University	L 2-8
1979	Michigan State	W 7-4
	Michigan Tech	L 4-5 3OT
1980	Michigan State	W 3-2
	Michigan Tech	L 2-3 OT
1981	Notre Dame	L 2-6
	Michigan State	T 4-4
1982	Michigan State	L 3-6
	Notre Dame	W 12-3
1983	Michigan Tech	L 4-5 OT
	Northern Michigan	L 3-5
1984	Michigan Tech	L 3-4
	Bowling Green	W 12-5
1985	Rensselaer	L 3-8
	Michigan Tech	W 6-4

Year	Opponent	Result		Year	Opponent	Result	
1986	Michigan Tech	W	4-3 OT	1998	Michigan Tech	W	4-1
	Western Michigan	L	2-8		Michigan State	L	1-3
1987	Wisconsin	L	0-6	1999	Lake Superior State	W	4-3 OT
	Michigan Tech	W	7-3		Michigan State	L	1-3
1988	Michigan Tech	W	7-3	2000	Michigan Tech	L	3-7
	North Dakota	W	6-5 2OT		Boston College	L	5-8
1989	Northern Michigan	W	7-1	2001	North Dakota	L	4-5 OT
	Michigan State	W	6-3		Michigan Tech	W	7-4
1990	Michigan Tech	W	2-1	2002	Michigan Tech	W	5-3
	Maine	W	3-1		Boston University	L	4-5
1991	Harvard	W	3-1	2003	Boston College	L	1-4
	Michigan Tech	W	7-1		Michigan Tech	W	6-2
1992	Michigan Tech	W	4-2	2004	Michigan Tech	W	4-2
	Northern Michigan	W	8-3		Michigan State	L	1-2 OT
1993	Notre Dame	W	8-3	2005	Colorado College	L	1-6
	Michigan State	W	4-2		Michigan Tech	W	5-3
1994	Michigan Tech	W	13-0	2006	Michigan Tech	W	4-1
	Michigan State	W	5-4		Michigan State	L	1-4
1995	Northern Michigan	W	6-1	2007	Providence	W	6-0
	Michigan State	W	3-1		Michigan Tech	W	1-0 2OT
1996	Michigan Tech	W	6-1	2008	Michigan Tech	W	5-0
	Lake Superior State	W	5-4		Michigan State	W	5-1
1997	St. Lawrence	W	3-2	2009	Rensselaer	L	4-3
	Michigan State	L	3-5		Michigan Tech	W	5-3

The Wolverines have made Detroit's Joe Louis Arena their personal "home away from home" since 1979 and continue to play in "the Joe" every year.

Home Away from Home

Having played 135 games (88-42-5) in Detroit's Joe Louis Arena, the Wolverines have made "the Joe" their unofficial home away from home since first defeating Michigan State 7-4 on December 28, 1979. Situated approximately 40 miles from Ann Arbor, 20,066-seat Joe Louis Arena is a hotbed for hockey greatness and hockey history. As the home of the NHL's Detroit Red Wings, the Joe has hosted everything from GLI and CCHA championships to NCAA and Stanley Cup championships.

The Wolverines visit Joe Louis Arena annually as one of the host schools for the Great Lakes Invitational hockey tournament.

Ice Chips

A Different Kind of Game

While Michigan's ice hockey team has had great success playing at Joe Louis Arena, the venue's inaugural event in 1979 had nothing to do with ice hockey. In fact, the first competition to be held in Joe Louis wasn't even ice hockey; it was a college basketball game featuring the University of Michigan. The Wolverines defeated the University of Detroit on December 12, 1979. Meanwhile, Joe Louis Arena's main tenant, the Detroit Red Wings, didn't host their first game until December 27, 1979. Another hockey game was played the following night—the very first Joe Louis Arena battle between Michigan and rival Michigan State University.

The Wolverines have stamped their ticket to the NCAA's Frozen Four an amazing 23 times, resulting in nine national championships.

Forever Frozen in Time

Although the NCAA has recognized a national ice hockey champion since Michigan captured the first ever title game in 1948, the tournament was not officially referred to as the "Frozen Four" until 1999. Of course, as the tournament continues to grow in popularity, so does the exposure and the size of the venue. While the first 10 national championship games were all played in Colorado Springs, Colorado, in front of fewer than 3,000 spectators, today's Frozen Four championship tournament is moved from city to city with games played in the nation's biggest and best venues. That changed in 2010 when the Frozen Four moved from a traditional arena setting to its largest venue yet: Detroit's domed football stadium, Ford Field. A record crowd of 37,592 watched Boston College defeat Wisconsin in the championship game. The 2010 Frozen Four marked the sixth time the championship event was played in Detroit, just a short drive from Michigan's Ann Arbor campus. It was also the third different venue in Detroit, including Olympia Stadium in 1977 and 1979 and Joe Louis Arena in 1985, 1987, and 1990.

Ice Chips

1-2-3-4-5-6-7-8-9!

The University of Michigan's ice hockey program has captured an NCAA record nine national championships. The Wolverines claimed the first Men's Ice Hockey Tournament in 1948 by defeating Dartmouth. That championship was merely a preview of things to come as Michigan went on to win five more national championships between 1951 and 1956 behind legendary coach Vic Heyliger. That on-ice domination was nearly duplicated from 1996 through 1998 when the Wolverines captured national titles in both 1996 and 1998 while advancing to the Frozen Four in 1997. Between 1990–91 and 1997–98, Michigan teams compiled a streak of winning at least 30 games during eight consecutive seasons while advancing to the Frozen Four on six occasions.

University of Michigan Ice Hockey National Champions: 1948, 1951, 1952, 1953, 1955, 1956, 1964, 1996, 1998

With 20 consecutive NCAA tournament appearances through 2009–10, Michigan continues to bounce its rivals year after year.

Always in the Hunt

Since those early heydays of the hockey program, the Wolverines have continued to consistently make their mark in both the national rankings and the annual NCAA ice hockey tournament. Michigan has made 33 appearances in the national tournament, including a current streak of 20 years in a row (1990–91 to 2009–10). Since their first national championship campaign in 1947–48, the Wolverines have placed teams in the NCAA final four in every decade except the 1980s while winning titles in five different decades under three different coaches.

Ice Chips

University of Michigan NCAA Tournament Success

- 23 championship round appearances
- 11 national championship game appearances
- 9 national championships
- 10 consecutive Frozen Four appearances (1948–57)
- 24 Frozen Four wins
- 20 consecutive NCAA tournament appearances
- 73 games played
- 47 games won

All-American Brendan Morrison put the icing on Michigan's 1996 national championship cake with a game-winning goal in overtime.

Working Overtime

Every championship season is filled with stories of heroics and extra effort. Michigan's last two national championships not only required extra effort but also extra time as both the 1996 and 1998 title games required a sudden-death, winner-take-all overtime period.

On March 30, 1996, the Wolverine's sensational forward Brendan Morrison poked in a rebound of Bill Muckalt's shot in overtime to lead Michigan to a 3-2 victory over Colorado College and notch UM's eighth national championship.

Michigan returned to the championship game again in 1998, and freshman Josh Langfeld sealed the Wolverine's ninth national title with a goal 17 minutes and 51 seconds into the first overtime to defeat Boston College at Boston's raucous Fleet Center. Langfeld was one of 11 freshmen who played that season for Michigan.

Ice Chips

A Record 35 Wins

While the 1996 and 1998 Michigan ice hockey teams brought home national championships, it was the 1997 team that racked up the highest single season win total in team history. Those Wolverines, led by Brendan Morrison and goaltender Marty Turco, compiled an astounding 35-4-4 record on their way to winning the CCHA championship while also advancing to the NCAA Frozen Four.

The Wolverines stamped their place in history by capturing the first NCAA Men's Ice Hockey Championship in 1948, defeating Dartmouth 8-4.

The First to Number One

On March 12, 1948, Coach Vic Heyliger brought the Wolverines to the Broadmoor Ice Palace in Colorado Springs, Colorado, for the first national championship game. Michigan broke open a 4-4 tie with four unanswered goals in the third period to defeat Dartmouth 8-4. Michigan received three goals and three assists from two-time All-American Wally Gacek and stout goaltending by Jack McDonald.

Ice Chips

Timing Is Everything

The 1948 championship game featured a disputed goal late in the second period when Michigan's Gordie McMillan scored to tie the game at 4-4. Playing long before the advent of today's precise electronic timers, the disputed play had been halted due to a timer's whistle. The timer was confused by a misunderstanding of the rules after Michigan's Al Renfrew went directly to the ice from the penalty box rather than reporting back to his bench first. Coach Heyliger disputed the call. The NCAA rules committee met during the second intermission and, ultimately, the goal was allowed.

Players and Coaches

In 2008, Kevin Porter became the second Wolverine to hoist the Hobey Baker Award, presented annually to college hockey's best player.

Hobey Baker—the Hockey Heisman

The definitive symbol of college hockey excellence, the Hobey Baker Memorial Award honors the memory of former Princeton hockey and football great, Hobey Baker. His unique skills, sportsmanship, and showmanship were evident anytime his skates touched the ice. Known for visiting the opponent's locker room after every game, Baker was penalized only once during his college hockey career—receiving a slashing penalty against Harvard in 1913. A WWII hero who shot down three German planes in dogfights, Baker's life was cut short at age 26 when he died testing a repaired aircraft. Yet the memories of his Hall of Fame hockey brilliance live on, and the 40-pound trophy in his name is made of bronze and clear, etched acrylic. Since 1981, the trophy has been awarded annually to college hockey's best player. A second trophy is also awarded to the winner's school.

Ice Chips

Gold Medal Standards

Elegantly detailed, the Hobey Baker Memorial Award trophy is the final work of a sculpture initially created from photographs of a skater stopping quickly, while sending ice shavings flying, and his stick and skates forming a three-point base. The model for the photos was Steve Christoff, a member of the Gold medal–winning USA hockey team that completed the Miracle on Ice in the 1980 Lake Placid Winter Olympics.

A three-time finalist, Brendan Morrison captured the coveted Hobey Baker Award in 1997 after leading Coach Red Berenson's team to the NCAA Frozen Four.

Hobey Baker Memorial Award Winner Brendan Morrison—1997

With a school record 284 career points and more than 100 goals as a Wolverine, Brendan Morrison was no stranger to big goals. Yet one goal stands apart from the rest. His overtime tally in the 1996 National Championship game vaulted Michigan to a heart-stopping 3-2 victory over Colorado College and captured the Wolverines' eighth NCAA title. Morrison also led the Wolverines into the 1997 Frozen Four. The high-flying center is one of only three Michigan players to be named All-American in three different seasons (1995, 1996, 1997) and twice he was named the CCHA Player of the Year (1996, 1997). A three-time finalist for the Hobey Baker Award, Morrison earned the ultimate collegiate hockey honor in 1997 after scoring 88 points in just 43 games.

Ice Chips

A Leader and the Best

During his Michigan career, Brendan Morrison (1994–97) set himself apart through his consistent excellence as a leader and a playmaker. As the university's all-time leading scorer in points and assists, he led the Wolverines in scoring three consecutive years and was named Michigan's MVP after both the 1996 and 1997 seasons.

In 1997–98, Morrison joined the NHL with the New Jersey Devils, scoring nine points in 11 games. The following season, he played 76 games and notched 46 points for the Devils. His NHL career has also featured stints with the Vancouver Canucks, Anaheim Ducks, Dallas Stars, and Washington Capitals. Morrison enjoyed his NHL career best season in 2002–03 when he scored 25 goals and 46 assists for Vancouver.

A stalwart on both ends of the ice, Kevin Porter was named college hockey's most outstanding player in 2008 after scoring 33 goals and 33 assists.

Hobey Baker Memorial Award Winner Kevin Porter—2008

As a senior in 2008, Kevin Porter was the consummate team player, leading the Wolverines in scoring while also being named a finalist for the CCHA's Best Defensive Forward. The captain and CCHA Player of the Year exemplified his leadership in the NCAA Regional Tournament by scoring five of Michigan's seven goals and adding an assist in helping the Wolverines into their record 23rd Frozen Four. Michigan came up short in its bid for a tenth national championship, but Porter captured the game's top individual award, winning the Hobey Baker trophy for his 33 goals and 33 assists in 43 games.

Ice Chips

Porter's Big Year

With 183 career points in 162 games for the Wolverines, Kevin Porter (2005–08) was a favorite amongst Michigan fans. But it was a stellar 2007–08 season that put Porter in the national spotlight as he led UM to a 20-4-4 record, a CCHA championship, and a spot in the Frozen Four. In addition to capturing the Hobey Baker Award, Porter earned a variety of other national player of the year honors. Originally drafted by the Phoenix Coyotes in the 2004 NHL Entry Draft, Porter joined the Coyotes and picked up an assist in his first NHL game against Columbus on October 11, 2008. He was traded to the Colorado Avalanche in March 2010.

The list of Wolverines garnering national attention by being named Hobey Baker finalists continues to grow.

Super Seasons

Brendan Morrison's exceptional career was highlighted by being named a Hobey Baker finalist for a Michigan-record three times: 1995, 1996, and 1997. Denny Felsner (1991, 1992) and T.J. Hensick (2005, 2007) were each named finalists on two occasions. Morrison won in 1997.

Ice Chips

Michigan's Hobey Baker Memorial Award Finalists

1991	Denny Felsner
1992	Denny Felsner
1994	David Oliver, Steve Shields, Brian Wiseman
1995	Brendan Morrison
1996	Brendan Morrison
1997	John Madden, Brendan Morrison
1998	Bill Muckalt
2000	Mike Comrie
2001	Andy Hilbert
2005	T.J. Hensick
2007	T.J. Hensick
2008	Kevin Porter
2009	Louie Caporusso

One of the earliest pioneers in UM hockey history, Eddie Kahn (sitting front center) also left a lasting impression on the University of Michigan's medical campus.

A Surgeon on the Ice

In 1923, Eddie Kahn helped pioneer the future of Michigan ice hockey by scoring the first official goal in Wolverine history. The goal came in the Wolverine's first varsity game against the University of Wisconsin on January 12, 1923, at the Weinberg Coliseum in Ann Arbor. It was Michigan's only goal in regulation play, but UM eventually won the inaugural contest 2-1, thanks to a goal by Robert Anderson during the second five-minute overtime period.

A fellow medical school student of then Michigan ice hockey coach Joseph Barss, Kahn captained the Wolverines team in 1924. Upon graduation in 1924, Kahn left the ice to become a medical pioneer and internationally acclaimed neurosurgeon. While he will forever be remembered for scoring the university's very first goal, Kahn's most lasting legacy comes from the 22 years he spent as Chief of Neurosurgery at the acclaimed University of Michigan Medical Center.

Ice Chips

Like Father, Like Son

Eddie Kahn's father, Albert Kahn, was a pioneer in his own right, a renowned architect who designed dozens of unique and groundbreaking buildings throughout Detroit as well as many buildings on the University of Michigan campus. His campus architectural handiwork includes Burton Tower, Angell Hall, West Engineering, National Science Building, the Graduate Library, Clements Library, as well as Ann Arbor's renowned Hill Auditorium, which opened in 1913 and remains one of the nation's premiere venues.

Michigan's all-time leader in coaching wins, Gordon "Red" Berenson has stood behind the UM bench as head coach since 1984.

Behind the Bench

Dozens of players have left a lasting legacy on the University of Michigan ice hockey program. Yet the list of coaches who have led this long-running program is much shorter. Joseph Barss helped establish the program in its infancy, leading the Wolverines to a 26-21-4 record between 1922–23 and 1926–27. However, it was the much longer tenures of Vic Heyliger (228 wins, six national championships), Al Renfrew (223 wins, one national championship), and Red Berenson (699 wins, two national championships through 2009–10) that cemented the Wolverines' place at the top of the collegiate hockey world.

Ice Chips

Michigan's All-Time Coaching Records

Joseph Barss	1922–23 to 1926–27	26-21-4
Edward Lower	1227–28 to 1943–44	124-136-21
Vic Heyliger	1944–45 to 1956–57	228-61-13
Al Renfrew	1957–58 to 1972–73	223-206-11
Dan Farrell	1973–74 to 1979–80	135-129-13
Wilf Martin	1980	1-1-1 (interim coach)
John Giardano	1980–81 to 1983–84	68-75-6
Red Berenson	1984–85 to present	699-328-69 (thru 2009–10)

Before taking the Michigan coaching reigns, Red Berenson led the Wolverines on the ice as a captain and two-time MVP and All-American.

Seeing Red

Nothing epitomizes Maize & Blue hockey more than Red. Gordon "Red" Berenson, who directed Michigan to the 1996 and 1998 NCAA Championships along with 20 consecutive NCAA appearances and seven Frozen Four appearances, has led Michigan's ice hockey program for more than a quarter century as both a player and coach. As a player (1959–62), Red was a two-time Michigan MVP and a two-time All-American. He shares the Wolverines' record with 43 goals in a season and tallied 78 goals and 59 assists during his UM career. Berenson also excelled in the classroom, earning both undergraduate and graduate degrees from Michigan. Berenson played professionally in the NHL for 17 seasons, scoring 261 goals and adding 397 assists. He won the Stanley Cup in 1965 with Montreal. As a professional coach, Red was named NHL Coach of the Year in 1981 for the St. Louis Blues.

Ice Chips

Taking It to the Next Level

Berenson played his final game in a Wolverines uniform during the 1962 NCAA Consolation Game. After leading UM to a victory against St. Lawrence, Berenson was driven to Boston where he donned a Montreal Canadiens uniform and played his first NHL game against the Bruins in the Boston Garden the next night—becoming the first collegiate player to go straight from the collegiate ranks into the NHL.

From the earliest years to today, Michigan goaltenders have always ranked among the very best in the collegiate ranks.

Saving Grace

Opposing goalies who surrender a goal are typically greeted by Michigan's raucous crowds at Yost Arena with derisive chants of "Sieve, sieve, sieve! It's all your fault." But as the last line of defense for the Wolverines, Michigan's goalies have long proven to be among the very best in college hockey. From old-time greats like Hal Downes, Lorne Howes, and Paul Fricker to Steve Shields, Marty Turco, Al Montoya, Josh Blackburn, and Billy Sauer, goaltending has always been a proud and stout position of strength for the Wolverines. Yet one name stands alone atop the all-time Michigan win list and the NCAA all-time win list: Marty Turco. The stalwart netminder was drafted in the fifth round of the NHL entry draft in 1994 by the Dallas Stars. Still, he elected to play for UM. Over the next four seasons in Ann Arbor, he posted a 127-28-7 record, surpassing Steve Shields (111 wins) as the winningest goaltender in Michigan and NCAA history. More important, Turco was the backbone of the Wolverines' two national championships in 1996 and 1998.

Ice Chips

.905 x 4 = Consistency

Talk about consistent goaltending. Michigan's stalwart netminder, Josh Blackburn, portrayed the epitome of consistency throughout his Wolverines career. In winning a whopping 92 games between 1999 and 2002, Blackburn posted an identical save percentage of .905 for each of his four seasons in the net. His spectacular 2.29 career goals-against average also ranks first on the all-time list for Michigan goaltenders. A native of North Pole, Alaska, Blackburn calls Michigan his home today, and he remains a vital component of the hockey program through his ongoing efforts as a volunteer goaltending coach for the Wolverines.

Dozens of Wolverines like Brendan Morrison have parlayed their success in Ann Arbor into professional careers in the NHL.

Gateway to the NHL

Michigan hockey is not only a premiere collegiate program, but also a highly regarded stepping stone for entrance into the professional ranks of the National Hockey League. While Red Berenson was the first collegiate player to step from college right into an NHL uniform, the Wolverines continue to fill NHL rosters year after year. In 2009–10, Michigan led all college programs with more than 20 former Wolverines playing in at least one NHL game that season, including: Mike Brown, Mike Cammalleri, Andrew Cogliano, Mike Comrie, Andrew Ebbett, Dwight Helminen, T.J. Hensick, Andy Hilbert, Matt Hunwick, Jack Johnson, Mike Knuble, Mike Komisarek, John Madden, Al Montoya, Brendan Morrison, David Moss, Eric Nystrom, Jed Ortmeyer, Max Pacioretty, Kevin Porter, Jeff Tambellini, Marty Turco, Mike Van Ryn, and Aaron Ward.

Ice Chips

Hockey's Holy Grail

Johnny Sherf (1932–36) became the first American-born player in history to have his name engraved on the Stanley Cup as a member of the 1936-37 champion Detroit Red Wings. Other Wolverines who also have their names engraved on the Holy Grail of the National Hockey League include Berenson, Aaron Ward, John Madden, Pat Hughes, Mike Knuble, and Blake Sloan.

Whether saluting a Michigan player's hat trick or some other outstanding play by the home team, the UM Ice Hockey Pep Band adds excitement with their efferves-cent presence.

Hats Off to You

The hat trick remains one of hockey's ultimate feats: three goals by one player in a single game. The term is thought to have originally derived from the sport of cricket when a bowler dismissed three batsmen with consecutive deliveries. That accomplishment was thought to entitle the individual to be presented with a new hat by his club. Today, a hockey hat trick is typically rewarded with the act of fans littering the ice rink with a deluge of hats whenever a player completes the three-goal achievement. Michigan's Dave Debol completed the fastest hat trick in Wolverines history on February 7, 1976, when he scored three times in a mere 59 seconds against Michigan Tech University. The most prolific hat trick performer for Michigan was Red Berenson who scored a team record nine hat tricks in 1961–62 and 10 during his UM career (1960–62). Debol (1975–78) and Gil Burford (1949–51) also scored hat tricks 10 times in their careers.

Ice Chips

Let's Make a Deal

The hockey hat trick is generally considered to have originated in 1946 when Alex Kaleta of the Chicago Black Hawks entered a local Toronto store looking to purchase a new hat. He didn't have enough money, but store owner Sammy Taft arranged a deal stipulating that if Kaleta scored three goals against the Toronto Maple Leafs that night, he would receive a free hat. Kaleta did him one better, scoring four goals, and afterward, Taft made good on the offer.

Shots on Goal

Michigan has been well represented in world and Olympic hockey competition. The Wolverines' 1966 team captain, Mel Wakabayashi, later coached Japan in the 1980 Olympic Games.

The World Is Watching

Hockey is truly an international sport with players coming from the U.S. and Canada as well as all over Europe and beyond. Of course, that global visibility is most evident during the Winter Olympic Games and other international competitions. The University of Michigan has long been well represented in those worldwide games. Wolverines Willard Ikola and John Matchefts both earned Silver Medals while skating for the U.S. ice hockey team at the 1956 Winter Olympic Games in Cortina d'Ampezzo, Italy, while UM teammate Bob White garnered a Bronze Medal with the Canadian Olympic team. Todd Brost (Silver, 1992) and David Harlock (Silver, 1994) also captured Olympic medals while playing for Team Canada. Most recently, Jack Johnson medaled (Silver, 2010) while playing for Team USA in the Winter Olympic Games played in Vancouver, British Columbia.

Ice Chips

Wolverines in the Winter Olympics (Ice Hockey)

1956	Willard Ikola, United States (Silver medalist)
	John Matchefts, United States (Silver medalist)
	Bob White, Canada (Bronze medalist)
1980	Mel Wakabayashi, Coach, Japan
1988	Jeff Norton, United States
1992	Todd Brost, Canada (Silver medalist)
1994	David Roberts, United States
	David Harlock, Canada (Silver medalist)
2006	Mike Knuble, United States
	Marty Turco, Canada
2010	Jack Johnson, United States (Silver medalist)

Quinnipiac is one of the many small universities around the nation that traditionally turn out high-level hockey programs.

Where in the World is Quinnipiac?

While Michigan's storied football program regularly competes against the biggest universities in the nation, the Wolverines welcome a variety of lesser known hockey powers to Yost Arena. In addition to traditional foes like Michigan State, Ohio State, and Minnesota, college hockey at Michigan provides high-quality opponents from universities with less famous names, including Lake Superior State, North Dakota, Alaska Anchorage, Nebraska at Omaha, Quinnipiac, Colorado College, Northeastern, Providence, Rensselaer, St. Lawrence, and Ferris State University.

Ice Chips

Connecticut Is Correct

Just 90 minutes from New York City and two hours from Boston, Quinnipiac University is situated next to picturesque Sleeping Giant Mountain in Hamden, Connecticut. The campus is home to approximately 5,700 undergraduates and 2,000 graduate students. The Bobcats of the Eastern College Athletic Conference (ECAC) have played NCAA Division 1 ice hockey since the 1998–99 season. Quinnipiac and Michigan have faced off four times in history, with the Wolverines winning each time.

In 1989, Coach Red Berenson incorporated UM's legendary and vaunted winged helmet design from football into the Michigan ice hockey helmets.

Wearing the Winged Helmet

When it's time to take the ice, Michigan's opponents are immediately greeted by the same daunting winged helmet made famous by the University of Michigan football team. The iconic design is unmistakably Michigan and instantly recognizable throughout the nation. The Wolverines' football team started wearing the winged helmet designed by Coach Herbert "Fritz" Crisler in 1938. However, it wasn't until February of 1989 that Michigan hockey coach Red Berenson approved the switch from plain white helmets to the now famous blue helmets with a maize "wing."

Ice Chips

Cover Your Head

The first player credited with wearing an ice hockey helmet was George Owen of the NHL's Boston Bruins back in 1928. Owen had played football at Harvard and continued to wear his leather football helmet when he joined the NHL. Helmets were seldom used until Bill Masterson of the Minnesota North Stars struck his head on the ice during a game on January 13, 1968, and died two days later. The tragedy led to a number of players wearing helmets and, by the 1970s, it was mandatory for college hockey players to wear helmets. Today's collegiate players are required to wear a helmet with a full cage or face guard.

Long, tedious road trips, poor ice conditions, and other obstacles limited the 1924–25 Wolverines to a six-game season.

A Six-Game Season

Today's Wolverines regularly play more than 40 games per season, including 28 conference games, against a wide variety of opponents from across the country. However, the early years of Michigan hockey featured schedules that were quite different. With few schools fielding teams, traveling to games could be long and grueling. Even after hours of travel, weather conditions could melt or diminish the ice surface and force the cancellation of games. The 1924–25 was the shortest on record, yielding a grand total of only 6 games. Coach Joe Barss' team opened the season with a loss to L'Assumption on January 16 in the team's one and only home game before defeating Michigan State University on January 24. The Wolverines traveled to Wisconsin on February 27–28, beating the Badgers 2-0 and 1-0. The team then trekked from Wisconsin to Minnesota where they tied the Golden Gophers 1-1 on March 2 before concluding the season with a 1-0 victory on March 3.

Ice Chips

Short Seasons

The 1925–26 Wolverines played only 10 games against three opponents: Michigan State, Minnesota, and Wisconsin. The 1944–45 Michigan team coached by Vic Heyliger played just nine games while facing off against foes that included the Detroit Vickers, Minnesota, Point Edwards, Brantford, Waterloo, London, and Middlesex-Huron. That season featured only one road game, at Minnesota.

Since 1925, backyard rivals Michigan and Michigan State University have faced off more than 270 times in ice hockey showdowns.

Rip-Roaring Rivalries

Michigan vs. Michigan State. These two backyard rivals have faced off against one another since the Wolverines defeated the Spartans 6-3 in their first ice hockey meeting on January 24, 1925. Today, these familiar foes have played more than 270 times throughout their storied histories. While Michigan's in-state competition with Michigan State is renewed only once per season on the football field, the Michigan-MSU ice hockey rivalry peaks on a number of occasions each season. In addition to CCHA league and playoff games, the Wolverines and Spartans can also meet in the Great Lakes Invitational or even the NCAA tournament. It is not uncommon for the teams to renew on-ice acquaintances five or six times in a season.

The Wolverines first played the University of Minnesota in ice hockey on January 23 and 24, 1923. That rivalry also continues to sizzle, with the teams having played 259 times through the 2009–10 season. While the teams now compete in different conferences, they still meet at least once each season in the College Hockey Showcase.

Ice Chips

A Packed House

The attraction of a rival game is evident in that each of the top single game home crowds in Michigan hockey history all came with Michigan State University visiting Yost Arena. Although the current configuration of Yost is listed at 6,637, the capacity was 8,100 between 1973–74 and 1991–92. The Wolverines and Spartans drew a record crowd of 8,411 on January 29, 1988. That figure was nearly matched a year later when 8,404 watched UM host MSU on February 18, 1989.

A powerful 1964 Michigan team racked up the most lopsided victory in UM hockey history by hammering rival Ohio State, 21-0.

A Three-Touchdown Victory

Michigan 21
Ohio State 0

The Wolverines traveled to Columbus to face Ohio State University on February 8, 1964, and trounced the Buckeyes, 21-0. In this case, this football-like score resulted in the most lopsided *hockey* victory in Michigan history. That 1964 Michigan powerhouse team compiled a 24-4-1 record under the leadership of Coach Al Renfrew and team captain Gordon Wilkie. The Wolverines captured both the Big Ten title and the WCHA regular season championships that season before sweeping past Providence and Denver in the NCAA championship round to win Michigan's seventh national championship.

Ice Chips

Turning the Tables

All odds favored Michigan when the Wolverines took on Denver in the WCHA championship game played at home in Ann Arbor on March 14, 1964. However, it was the Pioneers of Denver who skated away with a 6-2 victory over Michigan. Both teams advanced to NCAA tournament play and, as odds would have it, the two teams met again in the national championship game just one week later, this time in Denver. With everything on the line, Michigan turned the tables and defeated Denver, 6-3, led by two goals each from Jack Cole and Mel Wakabayashi.

The Dekers Blue Line Club has supported the Michigan hockey program since 1962 with a variety of events such as the annual Reunion game.

A-maizing Year-Round Support

When it comes to supporting Michigan Ice Hockey, one group stands alone at the top, the Dekers Blue Line Club. Established in 1962 with 25 inaugural members, the non-profit organization today boasts more than 750 active members and a variety of annual activities, events, and projects designed to support the University of Michigan hockey program. From a Labor Day picnic, alumni weekend, and golf outing to providing rings to graduating seniors and producing the popular *Inside the Goal Crease* newsletter, the Dekers Club is a prominent source of continued pride for Michigan hockey. The Dekers Club also became the first booster club in school history to endow a scholarship, providing room-and-board costs for one player each school year.

The Michigan Hall of Honor, established in 1978, recognizes those who have made significant contributions as athletes, coaches, and administrators to the tradition of Wolverine athletics and who, in doing so, have enhanced the University's image and reputation. Those inducted into the Hall of Honor have earned All-America recognition in a team or individual sport or as individuals have established a record, won an NCAA title, or made significant contributions to the Michigan Athletic Department as a coach or administrator. From 1990 to 2006, inductions were made every two years.

The Dekers Blue Line Club was organized in 1962 for the purpose of supporting the University of Michigan ice hockey program, while increasing public awareness of the program's great traditions.

Ice Chips

Dekers Blue Line Club

UM Hall of Honor

1980 Vic Heyliger
1981 John Sherf
1982 Jack Tompkins
1983 Red Berenson
1985 Connie Hill
1986 Al Renfrew
1987 Wally Grant
1989 Gordon Wilkie
1990 Willard Ikola
1992 Gordon McMillan
1994 John MacInnes
1996 Dave Debol
2004 Robert White
2006 Mel Wakabayashi
2007 Wally Gacek

Dekers Hall of Fame

Avon Artz
Larry Babcock
Doug Barnett
Joe Barss
Red Berenson
John Blum
Todd Brost
Gil Burford
Gary Butler
David Butts
Don Canham
Neil Celley
Ross Childs
Howard Colby
George Chin
Keith Crossman
Warren Crouch
Dave Debol
Paul Domm
Dick Dunnigan
Merle Falk
Greg Fox
Neil Gabler
Wally Gacek
Bernie Gagnon
Doug Galbraith
Paul Gamsby
Mickey Grant
Wally Grant
Bob Gray
Jim Haas
David Harlock
Bob Heathcott
Vic Heyliger
Connie Hill
Lorne Howes
Pat Hughes
Willard Ikola
Carl Isaacson
Eldon James
Gib James
John Jewell
Brad Jones
Steve Jones
Edgar Kahn
Jim Keough
Earl Keyes
Mike Knuble
Dan Lerg
Tom Lindskog

Bill Lord
Ed Lowrey
Dean Lucier
Joe Lunghamer
Dale MacDonald
Bill MacFarland
John MacInnes
Alex MacLellan
Kris Manery
Tim Manning
Joe Marmo
Wilf Martin
Mike Marttila
John Matchefts
Kip Maurer
John McDonald
John McKennell
Gordon McMillan
Mark Miller
Robbie Moore
Angie Moretto
Doug Mullen
Jeff Norton
Myles O'Connor
David Oliver
John Palenstein
Rob Palmer
Dan Petermann
Doug Philpott
Al Pickus
Bob Pitts
Rudy Reichert
Emerson Reid
Tom Rendall
Al Renfrew
David Roberts
Bob Schiller
Art Schlanderer
Warren Sharples
Reggie Shave
John Sherf
Steve Shields
George Sibilsky
Lois Simmons
Brian Skinner
Ross Smith
Ted Speers
Dick Starrak
Chris Tamer
Leonard Teitelbaum
Jack Tompkins
Randy Trudeau
Herb Upton
Mel Wakabayashi
Bob Watt
Bob White
Gordon Wilkie
Glenn Williams
Brian Wiseman

John Madden was more than a penalty killer, he was the opposition's worst power play nightmare as he scored 23 career short-handed goals.

Maddening to the Opposition

When playing short-handed, killing off the penalty time can boost a team's spirits and energize its play. Scoring while short-handed, on the other hand, can be downright disheartening for the opposition. Wolverine John Madden was a specialist in such demoralization. An extraordinary penalty killer, Madden scored an NCAA record 10 short-handed goals during the 1995–96 national championship season. He also tallied a NCAA record 23 short-handed goals over the course of his stalwart Michigan career—more than twice as many as any other Wolverine in history—and was an All-American in the 1996–97 season.

Ice Chips

Still Maddening

Following his Wolverines career, Madden took his exceptional penalty killing skills to the NHL where he immediately led the league and set a New Jersey Devils team record by scoring six short-handed goals during his rookie 1999–2000 season. On April 25, 2006, Madden capped off his first career NHL playoff hat trick by scoring two of his three goals while short-handed, tying another NHL record.

Michigan's own version of the "Miracle on Ice" occurred in 1985 when UM upset a highly favored Russian national team, 5-4, at Yost Arena.

The Russians Are Coming

The 1980 U.S. Olympic hockey team's stunning victory over the Soviet Union will forever be remembered as the Miracle on Ice. Yet just a few years later, a tired and struggling UM ice hockey team found itself in a similar position as it faced off in an exhibition game against the USSR Spartak club in 1985. While the Wolverines were coming off back-to-back losses in which they surrendered 18 goals, the older and more experienced Spartak team had already beaten six of the best American college teams, including a thrashing of top-ranked Wisconsin.

Despite being heavy underdogs, Michigan kept the game close. With the clock winding down in the third period and the score tied 4-4, Wolverine Joe Lockwood flipped a shot into the upper right corner of the net, beating Spartak goaltender Sergei Goloshumov in the final minute of regulation. Michigan held off the Soviets during the final 30 seconds to set off an improbable victory celebration.

Ice Chips

International Relations

While the victory over the Russian Spartak club remains one of the most memorable moments, the Wolverines have a long history of international competition. Michigan has taken to the ice for exhibitions against a number of foreign national and Olympic teams including:

Czechoslovakia (L 9-1, 12/30/1985)
Kladno Czechs (L 5-3, 01/07/1976)
Moscow Dynamo (L 12-0, 01/1980)
Russian Olympic Team (L 7-3, 01/06/1959)
Japan (W 6-4, 12/31/1984)
Polish Olympic Team (L 9-2, 02/06/1980)
West Germany (W 5-2, 02/27/1962)
Team Canada (L 8-2, 11/01/1985; L 6-2, 11/02/1985; L 4-2, 01/07/1995)
U.S. Olympic Team (L 4-1, 01/11/1956; W 6-5, 10/31/1975; L 9-7, 11/01/1975).

Many Michigan hockey players have been recognized for their individual accomplishments, including more than 60 who were named to All-American teams, such as Jack Johnson in 2007.

Best of the Best

From the early years to today, Michigan's hockey talent has always shined brightest, even on the national stage. A total of 63 players have been named to the All-American teams for their brilliant on-ice performances. Yet three players in Michigan's storied history have been selected as All-Americans three times in their careers. Wally Grant led the Wolverines to their first national championship in 1948 while being named All-American in 1948, 1949, and 1950. Bill MacFarland helped Michigan to two national championships in 1955 and 1956 while being named All-American in 1954, 1955, and 1956. More recently, Brendan Morrison was honored as an All-American in 1995, 1996, and 1997 while providing the Wolverines with the 1996 National Championship on his game-winning goal in overtime.

Ice Chips

Michigan's All-Americans, First Team

1948 Wally Gacek, Wally Grant, Connie Hill
1949 Wally Gacek, Wally Grant, Connie Hill, Ross Smith, Dick Starrak
1950 Wally Grant, Ross Smith
1951 Gil Burford, Neil Celley, Hal Downes, Bob Heathcott, John Matchefts
1952 George Chin, Jim Haas, Earl Keyes, John McKennell, Doug Philpott, Reg Shave
1953 George Chin, Willard Ikola, John Matchefts, Alex MacLellan, Reg Shave
1954 Jim Haas, Bill MacFarland
1955 Mike Buchanan, Dick Dunnigan, Lorne Howes, Bill MacFarland, Tom Rendall, Bob Schiller
1956 Lorne Howes, Bill MacFarland, Bob Schiller
1958 Bob White
1959 Bob Watt, Bob White
1961 Red Berenson
1962 Red Berenson
1964 Tom Polonic, Gordon Wilkie
1965 Mel Wakabayashi
1968 Jim Keough

1974 Robbie Moore
1977 Dave Debol
1980 Murray Eaves
1981 Paul Fricker
1989 Myles O'Connor
1992 Denny Felsner
1994 David Oliver, Brian Wiseman
1995 Brendan Morrison
1996 Brendan Morrison
1997 John Madden, Brendan Morrison, Marty Turco
1998 Bill Muckalt
2000 Jeff Jillson
2001 Andy Hilbert
2002 Mike Cammalleri, Mike Komisarek
2005 T.J. Hensick
2007 T.J. Hensick, Jack Johnson
2008 Kevin Porter
2009 Louie Caporusso, Aaron Palushaj

Michigan's All-Americans, Second Team

1987 Brad Jones
1991 Denny Felsner, David Roberts
1993 Steve Shields
1994 Steve Shields
1995 Mike Knuble
1996 Kevin Hilton
1997 Jason Botterill
2000 Mike Comrie
2001 Mike Cammalleri, Jeff Jillson
2004 Al Montoya
2005 Jeff Tambellini
2007 Matt Hunwick
2008 Chad Kolarik

The Record Book

Team Records/Awards

All-Time Annual Records

Overall

Year	GP	W	L	T
1922–23	11	4	7	0
1923–24	11	6	4	1
1924–25	6	4	1	1
1925–26	10	3	5	2
1926–27	13	9	4	0
1927–28	13	2	10	1
1928–29	17	5	11	1
1929–30	21	12	7	2
1930–31	17	10	5	2
1931–32	17	9	6	2
1932–33	16	10	4	2
1933–34	16	10	6	0
1934–35	17	12	3	2
1935–36	16	7	9	0
1936–37	18	11	6	1
1937–38	19	13	6	0
1938–39	18	8	8	2
1939–40	20	5	14	1
1940–41	17	2	14	1
1941–42	18	2	14	2
1942–43	13	1	10	2
1943–44	8	5	3	0
1944–45	9	3	6	0

Overall

Year	GP	W	L	T
1945–46	25	17	7	1
1946–47	21	13	7	1
1947–48	23	20	2	1
1948–49	25	20	2	3
1949–50	27	23	4	0
1950–51	27	22	4	1
1951–52	26	22	4	0
1952–53	24	17	7	0
1953–54	23	15	6	2
1954–55	24	18	5	1
1955–56	23	20	2	1
1956–57	25	18	5	2
1957–58	21	8	13	0
1958–59	22	8	13	1
1959–60	24	12	12	0
1960–61	28	16	10	2
1961–62	27	22	5	0
1962–63	24	7	14	3
1963–64	29	24	4	1
1964–65	26	13	12	1
1965–66	28	14	14	0
1966–67	28	19	7	2
1967–68	27	18	9	0

Overall

Year	GP	W	L	T
1968–69	28	16	12	0
1969–70	30	14	16	0
1970–71	30	9	21	0
1971–72	34	16	18	0
1972–73	34	6	27	1
1973–74	36	18	17	1
1974–75	40	22	17	1
1975–76	39	21	18	0
1976–77	45	28	17	0
1977–78	36	15	20	1
1978–79	36	8	27	1
1979–80	38	23	13	2
1980–81	40	23	17	0
1981–82	38	18	15	5
1982–83	36	14	22	0
1983–84	37	14	22	1
1984–85	40	13	26	1
1985–86	38	12	26	0
1986–87	40	14	25	1
1987–88	41	22	19	0
1988–89	41	22	15	4
1989–90	42	24	12	6

Overall

Year	GP	W	L	T
1990–91	47	34	10	3
1991–92	44	32	9	3
1992–93	40	30	7	3
1993–94	41	33	7	1
1994–95	39	30	8	1
1995–96	43	34	7	2
1996–97	43	35	4	4
1997–98	46	34	11	1
1998–99	42	25	11	6
1999–00	41	27	10	4
2000–01	45	27	13	5
2001–02	44	28	11	5
2002–03	43	30	10	3
2003–04	43	27	14	2
2004–05	42	31	8	3
2005–06	41	21	15	5
2006–07	41	26	14	1
2007–08	43	33	6	4
2008–09	41	29	12	0
2009–10	45	26	18	1

Michigan in the Frozen Four—Year-by-Year Results

Year	Champion	Runner Up	Third Place	Fourth Place
1948	MICHIGAN	Dartmouth	Colorado College, Boston College	—
1949	Boston College	Dartmouth	MICHIGAN	Colorado College
1950	Colorado College	Boston University	MICHIGAN	Boston College
1951	MICHIGAN	Brown	Boston University	Colorado College
1952	MICHIGAN	Colorado College	Yale	St. Lawrence
1953	MICHIGAN	Minnesota	Rensselaer	Boston University
1954	Rensselaer	Minnesota	MICHIGAN	St. Lawrence
1955	MICHIGAN	Colorado College	Harvard	St. Lawrence
1956	MICHIGAN	Mich. Tech	St. Lawrence	Boston College
1957	Colorado College	MICHIGAN	Clarkson	Harvard
1962	Michigan Tech	Clarkson	MICHIGAN	St. Lawrence
1964	MICHIGAN	Denver	Rensselaer	Providence
1977	Wisconsin	MICHIGAN	Boston University	New Hampshire
1992	Lake Superior	Wisconsin	MICHIGAN, Michigan State	
1993	Maine	Lake Superior	MICHIGAN, Boston University	
1995	Boston University	Maine	MICHIGAN, Minnesota	
1996	MICHIGAN	Colorado College	Vermont, Boston University	
1997	North Dakota	Boston University	MICHIGAN, Colorado College	
1998	MICHIGAN	Boston College	New Hampshire, Ohio State	
2001	Boston College	North Dakota	MICHIGAN, Michigan State	
2002	Minnesota	Maine	MICHIGAN, New Hampshire	
2003	Minnesota	New Hampshire	MICHIGAN, Cornell	
2008	Boston College	Notre Dame	MICHIGAN, North Dakota	

No consolation games played in 1948 and from 1990–present.

Michigan NCAA Tournament Results—Year-by-Year

1947–48 National Champions
Semifinal: Defeated Boston College, 6-4 (OT)
Championship: Defeated Dartmouth, 8-4

1948–49 Third Place
Semifinal: Lost to Dartmouth, 4-2
Third Place: Defeated Colorado College, 10-4

1949–50 Third Place
Semifinal: Lost to Boston University, 4-3
Third Place: Defeated Boston College, 10-6

1950–51 National Champions
Semifinal: Defeated Boston University, 8-2
Championship: Defeated Brown, 7-1

1951–52 National Champions
Semifinal: Defeated St. Lawrence, 9-3
Championship: Defeated Colorado College, 4-1

1952–53 National Champions
Semifinal: Defeated Boston University, 14-2
Championship: Defeated Minnesota, 7-3

1953–54 Third Place
Semifinal: Lost to RPI, 6-4
Third Place: Defeated Boston College, 7-2

1954–55 National Champions
Semifinal: Defeated Harvard, 7-3
Championship: Defeated Colorado College, 5-3

1955–56 National Champions
Semifinal: Defeated St. Lawrence, 2-1
Championship: Defeated Michigan Tech, 7-5

1956–57 Second Place
Semifinal: Defeated Harvard, 6-1
Championship: Lost to Colorado College, 13-6

1961–62 Third Place
Semifinal: Lost to Clarkson, 5-4
Third Place: Defeated St. Lawrence, 5-1

1963–64 National Champions
Semifinal: Defeated Providence, 3-2
Championship: Defeated Denver, 6-3

1976–77 Second Place
First Round: Defeated Bowling Green, 7-5
Semifinal: Defeated Boston University, 6-4
Championship: Lost to Wisconsin, 6-5 (OT)

1990–91 Quarterfinalist
First Round: Defeated Cornell, 2 games to 1 (4-5 [OT], 6-4, 9-3)
Quarterfinal: Lost to Boston University, 2 games to 0 (5-1, 8-1)

1991–92 Semifinalist
West Regional: Defeated Northern Michigan, 7-6
Semifinal: Lost to Wisconsin, 4-2

1992–93 Semifinalist
West Regional: Defeated Wisconsin, 4-3 (OT)
Semifinal: Lost to Maine, 4-3 (OT)

1993–94 Quarterfinalist
West Regional: Lost to Lake Superior State, 5-4 (OT)

1994–95 Semifinalist
West Regional: Defeated Wisconsin, 4-3
Semifinal: Lost to Maine, 4-3 (3OT)

1995–96 National Champions
West Regional: Defeated Minnesota, 4-3
Semifinal: Defeated Boston University, 4-0
Championship: Defeated Colorado College, 3-2 (OT)

1996–97 Semifinalist
West Regional: Defeated Minnesota, 7-4
Semifinal: Lost to Boston University, 3-2

1997–98 National Champions
West Regional: Defeated Princeton, 2-1
West Regional: Defeated North Dakota, 4-3
Semifinal: Defeated New Hampshire, 4-0
Championship: Defeated Boston College, 3-2 (OT)

1998–99 Quarterfinalist
East Regional: Defeated Denver, 5-3
East Regional: Lost to New Hampshire, 2-1 (OT)

1999–2000 Quarterfinalist
East Regional: Defeated Colgate, 4-3 (OT)
East Regional: Lost to Maine, 5-2

2000–01 Semifinalist
West Regional: Defeated Mercyhurst, 4-3
West Regional: Defeated St. Cloud State, 4-3
Semifinal: Lost to Boston College, 4-2

2001–02 Semifinalist
West Regional: Defeated St. Cloud State, 4-2
West Regional: Defeated Denver, 5-3
Semifinal: Lost to Minnesota, 3-2

2002–03 Semifinalist
Midwest Regional: Defeated Maine, 2-1
Midwest Regional: Defeated Colorado College, 5-3
Semifinal: Lost to Minnesota, 3-2 (OT)

2003–04 Quarterfinalist
Northeast Regional: Defeated New Hampshire, 4-1
Northeast Regional: Lost to Boston College, 3-2 (OT)

2004–05 Quarterfinalist
Midwest Regional: Defeated Wisconsin, 4-1
Midwest Regional: Lost to Colorado College, 4-3

2005–06 First Round
West Regional: Lost to North Dakota, 5-1

2006–07 First Round
West Regional: Lost to North Dakota, 8-5

2007–08 Semifinalist
East Regional: Defeated Niagara, 5-1
East Regional: Defeated Clarkson, 2-0
Semifinal: Lost to Notre Dame, 5-4 (OT)

2008–09 First Round
East Regional: Lost to Air Force, 2-0

2009–10 Quarterfinalist
Midwest Regional: Defeated Bemidji State, 5-1
Midwest Regional: Lost to Miami (OH), 3-2 (2 OT)

1948 NCAA Championship Game Summary

March 12, 1948, Colorado Springs, CO, Broadmoor Ice Palace (2,700)

Dartmouth	2	2	0—4	
Michigan	2	2	4—8	

1st period

UM—Wally Gacek (Wally Grant) 0:50
DC—Bill Riley (Bob Merriam) 4:25
UM—Gacek (Grant) 10:55
DC—Crawford Campbell (unassisted) 17:25 (PP)

2nd period

DC—Walt Crowley (B. Riley) 6:55
DC—Arnie Oss (Jim Malone) 11:05
UM—Grant (Gacek) 15:20
UM—Gordie McMillan (Ted Greer) 16:40

3rd period

UM—Grant (Gacek, Greer) 1:30
UM—McMillan (Al Renfrew) 6:15
UM—Gacek (Grant, Greer) 6:20
UM—Greer (Gacek) 15:14

Shots on goal

Dartmouth	12	9	8—29
UM	10	13	18—41

Penalties

Dartmouth 6-20
UM 8-16

Saves

Dartmouth Dick Desmond 33
UM John McDonald 25

1947–48 Team Roster

No.	Name	Pos.
1	John Griffin	D
2	Dick Starrak	D
3	Connie Hill	D
4	Leonard Brumm	F
5	Wally Gacek	F
6	Owen McArdle	F
7	Gordon McMillan	F
8	Bill Jacobson	F
9	Al Renfrew	F
10	Ted Greer	F
11	Herb Upton	D/F
12	Paul Milanowski	G
13	Sam Stedman	F
14	Ross Smith	D/F
15	Al Nadeau	F
16	Paul Fontana	F
17	John McDonald	G
17	Wally Grant	F
18	Bob Marshall	D
—	Bill Pritula	D

Head Coach: Vic Heyliger

1951 NCAA Championship Game Summary

March 17, 1951, Colorado Springs, CO, Broadmoor Ice Palace (2,700)

Brown	0 0 1—1
Michigan	2 3 2—7

1st period

UM—Eddie May (Gordon Naylor, Joe Marmo) 3:49

UM—Gil Burford (Alex MacLellan) 15:24

2nd period

UM—Neil Celley (unassisted) 6:41

UM—John McKennell (unassisted) 10:56

UM—Al Bassey (Earl Keyes, MacLellan) 14:19

3rd period

BU—Tony Malo (Bob Wheeler) 7:54

UM—McKennell (Burford, Keyes) 11:15

UM—Celley (Burford) 19:38

Shots on goal

BU	5	4	11—20
UM	17	21	14—52

Penalties

BU 2-4

UM 2-4

Saves

BU Don Whiston 45

UM Hal Downes 19

1950–51 Team Roster

No.	Name	Pos.
1	Hal Downes	G
3	Eddie May	D
4	John Matchefts	F
5	Bob Heathcott	D
6	Neil Celley	F
7	Earl Keyes	F
8	Gil Burford	F
9	Paul Pelow	F
10	John McKennell	F
11	Graham Cragg	D
12	Joe Marmo	F
14	Gordon Naylor	F
15	Al Bassey	F
18	Alex MacLellan	D

Head Coach: Vic Heyliger

1952 NCAA Championship Game Summary

March 15, 1952, Colorado Springs, CO, Broadmoor Ice Palace (2,500)

Michigan	3	1	0—4	
Colorado Coll.	0	1	0—1	

1st period

UM—George Chin (Doug Philpott) 11:35

UM—Earl Keyes (Jim Haas, Reg Shave) 16:29 (PP)

UM—Philpott (unassisted) 19:07 (SH)

2nd period

CC—Cameron Berry (Dick Kennific) 5:00

UM—Graham Cragg (Alex MacLellan) 10:12

3rd period

No scoring

Shots on goal

CC	10	13	9—32
UM	19	16	15—50

Penalties

CC 6-12

UM 7-22

Saves

CC Ken Kinsley 46

UM Willard Ikola 31

1951–52 Team Roster

No.	Name	Pos.
1	Willard Ikola	G
1	Bill Lucier	G
2	Jim Haas	D
3	Eddie May	F
4	John Matchefts	F
5	Bob Heathcott	D
6	George Chin	F
7	Earl Keyes	F
8	Pat Cooney	F
9	Paul Pelow	F
10	John McKennell	F
11	Graham Cragg	D
12	Doug Philpott	F
14	Gordon Naylor	F
15	Ron Martinson	F
17	Reg Shave	D
18	Alex MacLellan	D
19	Doug Mullen	F
—	Bob Lotzer	F
—	Telly Mascarin	F

Head Coach: Vic Heyliger

1953 NCAA Championship Game Summary

March 14, 1953, Colorado Springs, CO, Broadmoor Ice Palace (2,700)

Minnesota	2	0	1—3
Michigan	1	2	4—7

1st period

UM—Jim Haas (Alex MacLellan) 5:48

MIN—Dick Meredith (Ken Yackel) 8:39

MIN—Dick Dougherty (Gene Campbell) 11:34

2nd period

UM—Doug Philpott (Reg Shave) 6:15

UM—Doug Mullen (George Chin, Pat Cooney) 11:08

3rd period

UM—John Matchefts (unassisted) 3:38 (PP)

UM—Haas (unassisted) 7:17

UM—Philpott (Haas) 9:14 (PP)

MIN—Yackel (Robert Johnson, Dougherty) 10:42

UM—Matchefts (Philpott) 19:49 (EN)

Shots on goal

MIN	12	10	6—28
UM	14	11	9—34

Penalties

MIN 2-4

UM 6-12

Saves

MIN Jim Mattson 28

UM Willard Ikola 25

1952–53 Team Roster

No.	Name	Pos.
1	Willard Ikola	G
1	Bill Lucier	G
2	Jim Haas	D
4	John Matchefts	F
5	Burt Dunn	D
6	George Chin	F
7	Earl Keyes	F
8	Pat Cooney	F
10	John McKennell	F
12	Doug Philpott	F
14	Telly Mascarin	F
15	Ron Martinson	F
16	Louis Paolatto	D
17	Reg Shave	D
18	Alex MacLellan	D
19	Doug Mullen	F

Head Coach: Vic Heyliger

1955 NCAA Championship Game Summary

March 12, 1955, Colorado Springs, CO, Broadmoor Ice Palace (2,700)

Colorado Coll.	1	0	2—3
Michigan	2	0	3—5

1st period

UM—Tom Rendall (unassisted) 2:38

CC—Unknown

UM—Neil Buchanan (Mike Buchanan) 19:23

2nd period

No scoring

3rd period

UM—Jay Gould (unassisted) 6:18

CC—Don Wishart (Bunt Hubchik) 7:34

UM—Jerry Karpinka (Dick Dunnigan) 8:31

CC—Clare Smith (Doug Silverberg) 17:23

UM—Bill MacFarland (unassisted) 19:57 (EN)

Shots on goal

CC	12	15	23—50
UM	9	6	11—26

Penalties

CC 8-16

UM 9-18

Saves

CC Jeff Simus 22

UM Lorne Howes 47

1954–55 Team Roster

No.	Name	Pos.
1	Lorne Howes	G
2	Mike Buchanan	D
3	Bob Schiller	D
4	Bernie Hanna	D
5	Bob Pitts	D
6	Dick Dunnigan	F
7	Bill MacFarland	F
8	Jerry Karpinka	F
9	Jay Gould	F
10	Yves Hebert	F
11	Neil Buchanan	F
12	Tom Rendall	F
15	Baden Cosby	F
16	Bill Lucier	G

Head Coach: Vic Heyliger

1956 NCAA Championship Game Summary

March 17, 1956, Colorado Springs, CO, Broadmoor Ice Palace (2,800-est.)

Michigan Tech	3	2	0—5
Michigan	4	3	0—7

1st period

UM—Ed Switzer (Neil McDonald) 0:23

MTU—Dick Wilson (Jack McManus) 2:42

UM—McDonald (Bob Schiller) 9:22

UM—Don McIntosh (Tom Rendall) 10:14

MTU—Pete Aubry (unassisted) 11:04

UM—Schiller (McDonald) 13:11

MTU—Wilson (unassisted) 19:45

2nd period

MTU—Tom Kennedy (Wilson) 4:47

MTU—Aubry (Wilson) 7:25 (PP)

UM—Switzer (Bernie Hanna) 7:58

UM—Switzer (Dick Dunnigan) 14:28 (PP)

UM—McDonald (unassisted) 14:49

3rd period

No scoring

Shots on goal

MTU	22	10	10—42
UM	14	14	11—39

Penalties

MTU 5-13

UM 5-13

Saves

MTU Bob McManus 32

UM Lorne Howes 37

1955–56 Team Roster

No.	Name	Pos.
1	Lorne Howes	G
2	Mike Buchanan	D
3	Bob Schiller	D
4	Bernie Hanna	D
5	Bob Pitts	D
6	Dick Dunnigan	F
7	Bill MacFarland	F
8	Jerry Karpinka	F
9	Jay Gould F	
10	Wally Maxwell	F
11	Neil Buchanan	D
12	Tom Rendall	F
14	Don McIntosh	F
15	Neil McDonald	F
16	Morley Chin	F
17	Ed Switzer	F

Head Coach: Vic Heyliger

1964 NCAA Championship Game Summary

March 21, 1964, Denver, CO, University of Denver Arena (5,296)

	1	2	3	Final
Michigan	1	2	3	6
Denver	0	2	1	3

1st period

UM—Wilf Martin (Alex Hood, Tom Polonic) 17:48

2nd period

UM—Mel Wakabayashi (Bob Ferguson, Gordon Wilkie) 2:19 (PP)

UM—Jack Cole (Wilkie) 3:22

DU—Billy Staub (Andy Herrebout, Bob Lindsay) 5:34 (PP)

DU—Ron Livingstone (Emory Sampson, Ron Naslund) 17:24

3rd period

UM—Cole (Polonic, Wilkie) 4:08

DU—Wayne Smith (Herrebout) 9:54 (PP)

UM—Wakabayashi (Ron Coristine, Ferguson) 16:49

UM—Hood (Polonic, Martin) 18:24

Shots on goal

DU	15	10	9—34
UM	7	6	16—29

Penalties

DU 5-10

UM 11-30

Saves

DU Buddy Blom 23

UM Bob Gray 31

Power Plays

DU 2-9

UM 1-3

1963–64 Team Roster

No.	Name	Pos.
1	Bill Bieber	G
1	Bob Gray	G
2	Tom Polonic	D
3	Ted Henderson	D
4	Rick Day	D
5	Pierre Dechaine	F
6	Jack Cole	F
7	Wilf Martin	F
8	Alex Hood	F
9	Mel Wakabayashi	F
10	Bob Ferguson	F
11	Roger Galipeau	D
12	Ron Coristine	F
13	Barry MacDonald	F
14	George Forrest	F
16	Marty Read	F
17	Dave Newton	D
18	Gary Butler	F
19	Gordon Wilkie	F

Head Coach: Al Renfrew

1996 NCAA Championship Game Summary

March 30, 1996, Cincinnati, OH, Riverfront Coliseum (12,957)

Michigan	1 0 1 1—3
Colorado College	0 2 0 0—2

1st period

UM - Bill Muckalt (Brendan Morrison) 11:33

2nd period

CC—Peter Geronazzo (Colin Schmidt, Eric Rud) 3:52 (PP)

CC—Schmidt (Geronazzo, Chad Remackel) 5:37

3rd period

UM—Mike Legg (Steven Halko, Harold Schock) 6:54 (PP)

Overtime

UM—Morrison (Muckalt, Greg Crozier) 3:35

Shots on goal

CC 5 8 9 1—23

UM 3 4 10 2—19

Penalties

CC 10-20

UM 10-20

Saves

CC Ryan Bach 16

UM Marty Turco 21

Power Plays

CC 1-5

UM 1-5

1995–96 Team Roster

No.	Name	Pos.
2	Mark Sakala	D
3	Bubba Berenzweig	D
4	Chris Frescoln	D
5	Peter Bourke	D
6	Harold Schock	D
7	Justin Clark	F
8	Matt Herr	F
9	Brendan Morrison	F
10	Kevin Hilton	F
13	Greg Crozier	F
14	Craig Assenmacher	F
15	Mike Legg	F
16	Bill Muckalt	F
17	Sean Ritchlin	F
18	John Madden	F
19	Jason Botterill	F
20	John Arnold	F
23	Dale Rominski	F
24	Steven Halko	D
25	Bobby Hayes	F
26	Chris Fox	D
27	Blake Sloan	D
28	Warren Luhning	F
29	Gregg Malicke	G
30	Greg Daddario	G
35	Marty Turco	G

Head Coach: Red Berenson

1998 NCAA Championship Game Summary

April 4, 1998, Boston, MA, Fleet Center (18,276)

Michigan	0 1 1 1—3
Boston Coll.	1 1 0 0—2

1st period

BC—Kevin Caulfield (Mike Mottau) 4:19

2nd period

UM—Mark Kosick (Bubba Berenzweig, Greg Crozier) 7:42

BC—Mike Lephart (Jeff Farkas, Bobby Allen) 18:38 (PP)

3rd period

UM—Kosick (Bill Muckalt, Chris Fox) 13:48

Overtime

UM—Josh Langfeld (Fox, Scott Matzka) 17:51

Shots on goal

BC 11 7 9 3—30

UM 7 8 10 10—35

Penalties

BC 6-12

UM 5-10

Saves

BC Scott Clemmensen 32

UM Marty Turco 28

Power Plays

BC 1-4

UM 0-5

1997–98 Team Roster

No.	Name	Pos.
2	Kevin Magnuson	D
3	Bubba Berenzweig	D
4	Mike Van Ryn	D
6	Scott Crawford	D
7	Justin Clark	F
8	Matt Herr	F
9	Mark Kosick	F
10	Scott Matzka	F
11	Andrew Merrick	F
16	Bill Muckalt	F
17	Sean Ritchlin	F
18	Geoff Koch	F
20	Bob Gassoff	D
21	Josh Langfeld	F
22	Bill Trainor	F
23	Dale Rominski	F
24	Sean Peach	D
25	Bobby Hayes	F
26	Chris Fox	D
27	David Huntzicker	D
29	Gregg Malicke	G
30	Greg Daddario	G
32	Krikor Arman	F
33	Greg Crozier	F
35	Marty Turco	G

Head Coach: Red Berenson

Overall Winning Streaks

Games	Began / vs.	Ended / vs.
15 (2 seasons)	3/1/96 MSU	11/2/96 MSU
15	12/28/90 MTU	2/16/91 MSU
14 (2 seasons)	2/16/52 Colorado College	12/23/53 Denver
12	10/19/07 NMU	11/30/07 Ohio State
12	2/11/77 Denver	3/16/77 Wisconsin
12	1/17/64 Loyola (Mtl.)	2/28/64 MTU
12 (2 seasons)	2/8/56 Colorado College	12/10/56 Toronto
12 (2 seasons)	2/11/55 MSU	12/10/55 North Dakota

Home Winning Streaks

Games	Began / vs.	Ended / vs.
17 (2 seasons)	1/15/93 OSU	1/21/94 MSU
17 (2 seasons)	3/3/61 MSU	3/3/62 MTU
15 (2 seasons)	1/7/50 Montreal	1/12/51 Montreal
12	10/20/79 BGSU	1/12/80 Colorado College
12	12/14/63 Toronto	3/13/64 MTU

Road Winning Streaks

Games	Began / vs.	Ended / vs.
9	11/5/93 LSSU	2/25/94 Miami
9	12/7/90 WMU	3/22/91 Boston University
9 (2 seasons)	2/11/50 MTU	2/7/51 Denver
8	10/19/07 NMU	1/26/08 MSU
8	10/29/94 FSU	2/11/95 Illinois-Chicago

Overall CCHA Winning Streak

Games	Began / vs.	Ended / vs.
16	10/30/93 Notre Dame	1/21/94 MSU
13	1/4/91 Illinois-Chicago	2/16/91MSU
12	11/5/04 Miami	1/21/05 OSU
12 (2 seasons)	1/26/02 BGSU	11/9/02 BGSU
10	11/21/97 BGSU	1/23/98 Miami

CCHA Home Winning Streak

Games	Began / vs.	Ended / vs.
22 (2 seasons)	10/24/03 NMU	1/28/05 NMU
16 (2 seasons)	3/1/96 MSU	2/22/97 LSSU
15 (2 seasons)	1/15/93 OSU	1/21/94 MSU
11 (2 seasons)	1/26/02 BGSU	11/23/02 Notre Dame
10	11/17/95 UAF	2/3/96 OSU

CCHA Road Winning Streak

Games	Began / vs.	Ended / vs.
10	11/17/90 LSSU	10/25/91 MSU
9	11/5/93 LSSU	2/25/94 Miami
8	10/19/07 NMU	1/26/08 MSU
8	10/29/94 FSU	2/11/95 Illinois-Chicago
7 (2 seasons)	3/3/95 Miami	11/28/95 MSU

Overall Unbeaten Streaks

Games (record)	Began / vs.	Ended / vs.
23 (20-0-3)	11/8/96 OSU	2/8/97 MSU
21 (18-0-3) (2 seasons)	2/16/48 California	1/31/49 MTU
16 (15-0-1)	12/15/90 LSSU	2/16/91 MSU
15 (15-0-0) (2 seasons)	3/1/96 MSU	11/2/96 MSU

Home Unbeaten Streaks

Games (record)	Began / vs.	Ended / vs.
36 (33-0-3) (3 seasons)	11/17/95 UAF	10/17/97 Colgate
19 (18-0-1) (3 seasons)	2/16/48 California	12/17/49 Toronto
18 (17-0-1) (3 seasons)	2/8/56 Colorado College	12/6/57 McGill
17 (17-0-0) (2 seasons)	1/15/93 OSU	1/21/94 MSU
17 (17-0-0) (2 seasons)	3/4/61 MSU	3/3/62 MTU

Road Unbeaten Streaks

Games (record)	Began / vs.	Ended / vs.
15 (14-0-1) (2 seasons)	2/13/93 BGSU	2/25/94 Miami
15 (12-0-3) (2 seasons)	11/2/01 Alaska	12/6/02 NMU
11 (9-0-2)	10/19/07 NMU	2/22/08 MSU
9 (6-0-3) (2 seasons)	1/7/00 MSU	11/11/00 FSU
9 (7-0-2) (2 seasons)	3/6/98 BGSU	1/2/99 OSU
9 (9-0-0)	11/5/93 LSSU	2/25/94 Miami
9 (9-0-0)	12/7/90 WMU	3/22/91 Boston University
9 (9-0-0) (2 seasons)	2/11/50 MTU	2/7/51 Denver
9 (8-0-1) (2 seasons)	1/16/48 Minnesota	1/31/49 MTU

Overall CCHA Unbeaten Streaks

Games (record)	Began / vs.	Ended / vs.
24 (23-0-1) (2 seasons)	2/13/93 BGSU	1/21/94 MSU
16 (15-0-1) (2 seasons)	1/26/02 BGSU	11/23/02 Notre Dame
16 (14-0-2)	11/8/96 OSU	2/8/97 MSU
16 (16-0-0)	10/30/93 Notre Dame	1/21/94 MSU
14 (13-0-1)	12/15/90 LSSU	2/16/91 MSU

CCHA Home Unbeaten Streaks

Games (record)	Began / vs.	Ended / vs.
28 (26-0-2) (3 seasons)	11/17/95 UAF	10/25/97 MSU
22 (22-0-0) (2 seasons)	10/24/03 NMU	1/28/05 NMU
16 (16-0-0) (2 seasons)	3/1/96 MSU	2/22/97 LSSU
15 (15-0-0) (2 seasons)	1/15/93 OSU	1/21/94 MSU
15 (13-0-2) (2 seasons)	1/11/91 Miami	2/8/92 BGSU

CCHA Road Unbeaten Streak

Games (record)	Began / vs.	Ended / vs.
13 (10-0-3) (2 seasons)	11/2/01 UAF	12/6/02 NMU
13 (12-0-1) (2 seasons)	2/13/93 BGSU	2/25/94 Miami
11 (9-0-2)	10/19/07 NMU	2/22/08 MSU
10 (10-0-0) (2 seasons)	11/17/90 LSSU	10/25/91 MSU
8 (6-0-2) (2 seasons)	1/7/00 MSU	11/11/00 FSU
8 (8-0-0)	10/29/94 FSU	2/11/95 UIC

Michigan Single Season Team Records

Most Wins	35	1996–97
Most Home Wins	19	2003–04
Most Road Wins	13	1990–91
Fewest Losses	2	1947–48, 1948–49, 1955–56
Fewest Road Losses	0	1947–48, 1951–52
Fewest Home Losses	0	1948–49, 1956–57, 1961–62, 1996–97
Most Ties	6	1989–90, 1998–99
Fewest Ties	0	18 seasons
Most Wins in a Month	9	Feb. 1948, Feb. 1954, Dec. 1961, Mar. 1996
Best Winning Percentage	.891	(20-2-1) 1947–48, 1955–56
Best Winning Pct. at Home	1.000	(12-0-0) 1961–62
Best Winning Pct. on Road	1.000	(4-0-0) 1947–48
Lowest Goals Against Avg	1.47	1930–31
Best Goals/Game Avg.	7.85	1950–51
Most Goals	260	1976–77
Most Short-Handed Goals	22	1996–97
Most Shutouts	9	1995–96

The Record Book

Individual Records/Awards

Game-Winning Goals

Season (Since 1967–68)

Mike Knuble	1994–95	8
Bill Muckalt	1997–98	8
David Oliver	1993–94	8
Dale Rominski	1998–99	8
Mike Cammalleri	2001–02	7
Andy Hilbert	2000–01	7
Chad Kolarik	2007–08	7
Kip Maurer	1976–77	7
Brian Wiseman	1991–92	7
Dave Debol	1975–76	6
Warren Luhning	1996–97	6
David Oliver	1992–93	6
Jeff Tambellini	2002–03	6
Brian Wiseman	1993–94	6

Career

David Oliver	1991–94	21
Bill Muckalt	1995–98	19
Chad Kolarik	2005–08	17
Denny Felsner	1989–92	16
Brian Wiseman	1991–94	16
Dave Debol	1975–78	15
Kevin Porter	2005–08	15
Mike Knuble	1992–95	14
Warren Luhning	1994–97	14
Jeff Tambellini	2003–05	14
Jason Botterill	1994–97	13
Matt Herr	1995–98	13

Points by a Defenseman (Goals + Assists)

Single Season

Steve Richmond	1980–81	54
John Blum	1980–81	52
Tim Manning	1979–80	51
John Blum	1979–80	50
Jeff Norton	1986–87	48
Tom Polonic	1963–64	46
Jeff Norton	1985–86	45
Myles O'Connor	1986–87	45
Bob Heathcott	1951–52	44
Tim Manning	1980–81	44

Career

Tim Manning	1978–81	142
Myles O'Connor	1986–89	138
Patrick Neaton	1990–93	127
Steve Richmond	1979–82	126
Jeff Norton	1985–87	117
John Blum	1978–81	114
Rob Palmer	1974–77	98
Matt Hunwick	2004–07	97
Tom Lindskog	1973–76	97
Harold Schock	1994–97	94

Power Play Goals

Season (Since 1967–68)

Mike Knuble	1993–94	21
Kip Maurer	1977–78	21
Jason Botterill	1996–97	20
Denny Felsner	1990–91	18
Dan Lerg	1979–80	18
Denny Felsner	1991–92	17
Bruno Baseotto	1979–80	16
Dave Debol	1976–77	16
David Oliver	1993–94	16
Steve Richmond	1980–81	16

Career

Denny Felsner	1989–92	60
David Oliver	1991–94	52
Jason Botterill	1994–97	50
Mike Knuble	1992–95	48
Bill Muckalt	1995–98	41
Dan Lerg	1977–80	38
Brendan Morrison	1994–97	37
Dave Debol	1975–78	34
Kip Maurer	1975–78	34
Kevin Porter	2005–08	32

Short-Handed Goals

Season (Since 1967–68)

John Madden	1995–96	10 *
John Madden	1996–97	8
Scott Matzka	1999–2000	6
Matt Herr	1996–97	5
Joe Lockwood	1986–87	5
Warren Luhning	1996–97	5
John Madden	1993–94	5
Bobby Hayes	1997–98	4
Dwight Helminen	2002–03	4
Chad Kolarik	2007–08	4

Career

John Madden	1994–97	23 *
Matt Herr	1995–98	9
Warren Luhning	1994–97	9
Scott Matzka	1998–2001	8
Dwight Helminen	2002–04	7
Dan Hoene	1975–78	7
Chad Kolarik	2005–08	7
Geoff Koch	1998–2001	6
Bobby Hayes	1996–99	6
Dale Rominski	1996–99	6
Rob Brown	1987–90	6
Joe Lockwood	1985–88	6
Brad Tippett	1980–83	6

*NCAA Record

Goals

Single Season

Red Berenson	1961–62	43
Dave Debol	1976–77	43
Denny Felsner	1991–92	42
Gil Burford	1949–50	40
Neil Celley	1950–51	40
Denny Felsner	1990–91	40
Angie Moretto	1974–75	39
Gary Butler	1963–64	38
Mike Knuble	1994–95	38
Kris Manery	1976–77	38
Kip Maurer	1976–77	38

Career

Denny Felsner	1989–92	139
Neil Celley	1946, 49–51	119
Dave Debol	1975–78	112
Kris Manery	1974–77	111
David Oliver	1991–94	107
Bill Muckalt	1995–98	105
Jason Botterill	1994–97	104
Gil Burford	1949–51	103
Mike Knuble	1992–95	103
Brendan Morrison	1994–97	102

Assists

Single Season

Brendan Morrison	1996–97	57
Dave Debol	1976–77	56
Brendan Morrison	1994–95	53
Denny Felsner	1991–92	52
Kevin Hilton	1995–96	51
Gordon Wilkie	1963–64	51
Brian Wiseman	1993–94	50
Murray Eaves	1979–80	49
Brad Jones	1986–87	46
T.J. Hensick	2006–07	46

Career

Brendan Morrison	1994–97	182
Brian Wiseman	1991–94	164
David Roberts	1990–93	157
T.J. Hensick	2004–07	147
Brad Jones	1984–87	138
Dave Debol	1975–78	134
Mark Ouimet	1990–93	128
Denny Felsner	1989–92	122
Bill Muckalt	1995–98	121
Gordon McMillan	1946–49	114

Points (Goals + Assists)

Single Season

Dave Debol	1976–77	99
Denny Felsner	1991–92	94
Brendan Morrison	1996–97	88
Murray Eaves	1979–80	85
Neil Celley	1950–51	79
Brad Jones	1986–87	78
Bruno Baseotto	1979–80	76
Dan Lerg	1979–80	76
Kip Maurer	1976–77	76
Brendan Morrison	1994–95	76

Career

Brendan Morrison	1994–97	284
Denny Felsner	1989–92	261
Brian Wiseman	1991–94	248
David Roberts	1990–93	247
Dave Debol	1975–78	246
Brad Jones	1984–87	227
Bill Muckalt	1995–98	226
T.J. Hensick	2004–07	222
Neil Celley	1946, 49–51	215
Gordon McMillan	1946–49	213

Wins

Single Season

Marty Turco	1995–96	34
Marty Turco	1997–98	33
Marty Turco	1996–97	33
Al Montoya	2004–05	30
Al Montoya	2002–03	30
Steve Shields	1992–93	30
Billy Sauer	2007–08	30

Career

Marty Turco	1995–98	127 *
Steve Shields	1991–94	111
Josh Blackburn	1999–2002	92
Al Montoya	2003–05	86
Billy Sauer	2006–08	71

Shutouts

Single Season

Al Montoya	2003–04	6
Josh Blackburn	2001–02	5
Josh Blackburn	2000–01	5
Marty Turco	1995–98	5
Billy Sauer	2007–08	4
Al Montoya	2002–03	4
Marty Turco	1997–98	4
Marty Turco	1996–97	4
Bob Gray	1963–64	4

Career

Marty Turco	1995–98	15
Josh Blackburn	1999–2002	14
Al Montoya	2003–05	13
Billy Sauer	2006–09	8
Jim Keough	1967–69	7

*NCAA Record

Goals Against Average

Single Season

Billy Sauer	2007–08	1.95
Bryan Hogan	2008–09	1.97
Marty Turco	1995–96	2.16
Marty Turco	1997–98	2.16
Steve Shields	1992–93	2.22
Al Montoya	2003–04	2.23
Josh Blackburn	2001–02	2.24
Marty Turco	1996–97	2.27
Josh Blackburn	1998–99	2.28
Josh Blackburn	2000–01	2.29

Career

Josh Blackburn	1999–2002	2.29
Marty Turco	1995–98	2.32
Al Montoya	2003–05	2.36
Billy Sauer	2006–08	2.56
Steve Shields	1991–94	2.73

Games Played

Single Season

Josh Blackburn	2000–01	45
Marty Turco	1997–98	45
Josh Blackburn	2001–02	43
Al Montoya	2002–03	43
Marty Turco	1995–96	42
Josh Blackburn	1998–99	41
Marty Turco	1996–97	41
Al Montoya	2004–05	40
Al Montoya	2003–04	40
Billy Sauer	2006–07	40

Career

Marty Turco	1995–98	165
Josh Blackburn	1999–2002	151
Steve Shields	1991–94	149
Scott Sharples	1987–90	137
Robbie Moore	1973–76	128

Save Percentage

Single Season

Billy Sauer	2007–08	.924
Al Montoya	2003–04	.917
Bryan Hogan	2008–09	.9139
Bob Gray	1963–64	.9136
Al Montoya	2002–03	.911
Steve Shields	1992–93	.909
Jim Keough	1967–68	.908
Marty Turco	1997–98	.907
Jim Keough	1966–67	.9066
Josh Blackburn	2001–02	.905
Josh Blackburn	2000–01	.905
Josh Blackburn	1999–2000	.905
Josh Blackburn	1998–99	.905
Bob Gray	1961–62	.905

Career

Al Montoya	2003–05	.90806
Bob Gray	1962–64	.90798
Billy Sauer	2006–08	.90792
Josh Blackburn	1999–2002	.905
Jim Keough	1967–69	.901

Saves

Single Season

Karl Bagnell	1971–72	1,305
Robbie Moore	1972–73	1,254
Robbie Moore	1973–74	1,203
Rick Palmer	1976–77	1,191
Robbie Moore	1975–76	1,160
Paul Fricker	1979–80	1,122
Paul Fricker	1980–81	1,044
Billy Sauer	2006–07	1,028
Al Montoya	2002–03	1,014
Mark Chiamp	1983–84	1,002

Career

Robbie Moore	1973–76	4,434 *
Scott Sharples	1987–90	3,534
Josh Blackburn	1999–2002	3,250
Marty Turco	1991–94	2,990

*NCAA Record

Team Captains

1924	Edgar A. Kahn
1925	Dan Petermann
1926	Irving Reynolds
1927	Steve Jones
1928	Bill Maney
1929	Jim Fisher
1930	Clarence Bryant
1931	Art Schlanderer
1932	John Tompkins
1933	Emerson Reid
	Keith Crossman
1934	George David, Jr.
1935	John Sherf
	John Jewell
1936	Larry David
1937	Vic Heyliger
1938	Robert Simpson
1939	Leslie Hillberg
1940	Eldon James
1941	Charlie Ross
1942	Paul Goldsmith
1943	Henry Loud
1944	Bob Derleth
1945	Ted Greer
1946	Conrad Hill
1947	Conrad Hill
1948	Conrad Hill
1949	Al Renfrew
1950	Wally Grant
1951	Gil Burford
1952	Earl Keyes
1953	John Matchefts
1954	Jim Haas
1955	Bill MacFarland
1956	Bill MacFarland
1957	Bob Pitts
1958	Neil McDonald
1959	Bob Watt
1960	Bob Watt
1961	Dale MacDonald
1962	Red Berenson
1963	Larry Babcock
1964	Gordon Wilkie
1965	Wilf Martin
1966	Mel Wakabayashi
1967	Mike Marttila
1968	Bill Lord
1969	Paul Domm
1970	Dave Perrin
1971	Paul Gamsby
1972	Brian Skinner
1973	Rick Mallette
1974	Randy Trudeau
1975	Randy Trudeau
1976	Angie Moretto
	Tom Lindskog
	Greg Fox
1977	Kris Manery
1978	John McCahill
1979	Mark Miller
1980	Doug Todd
1981	Tim Manning
1982	Steve Richmond
	David Richter
1983	Ted Speers
	Brad Tippett
1984	Jim McCauley
	Kelly McCrimmon
1985	Ray Dries
1986	Frank Downing
1987	Jeff Norton
1988	Todd Brost
1989	Todd Brost
	Myles O'Connor
1990	Alex Roberts
	Mike Moes
1991	David Harlock
	Don Stone
1992	David Harlock
1993	David Harlock
1994	Brian Wiseman
1995	Rick Willis
1996	Steven Halko
1997	Brendan Morrison
1998	Matt Herr
1999	Bubba Berenzweig
2000	Sean Peach
2001	Geoff Koch
2002	Jed Ortmeyer
2003	Jed Ortmeyer
2004	Andy Burnes
2005	Eric Nystrom
2006	Andrew Ebbett
2007	Matt Hunwick
2008	Kevin Porter
2009	Mark Mitera
2010	Chris Summers

Hal Downes Trophy—Most Valuable Player

Presented to the season's most valuable player, as chosen by the members of the team. This trophy honors the memory of Hal Downes, a goaltender on the 1951 NCAA Championship team who was missing in action during the Korean War.

1956	Lorne Howes
1957	Dick Dunnigan
1958	Neil McDonald
1959	John Hutton
1960	Bob White
1961	Red Berenson
1962	Red Berenson
1963	Bob Gray
1964	Gordon Wilkie
1965	Mel Wakabayashi
1966	Mel Wakabayashi
1967	Bob Baird
	Dean Lucier
1968	Jim Keough
1969	Paul Domm, Lars Hansen
1970	Don Deeks
1971	Paul Gamsby
	Brian Skinner
1972	Karl Bagnell
	Bernie Gagnon
1973	Rick Mallette
1974	Robbie Moore
1975	Angie Moretto
1976	Kris Manery
1977	Dave Debol
1978	Ben Kawa
1979	Mark Miller
1980	Paul Fricker
1981	John Blum
	Tim Manning
1982	Ted Speers
1983	Ted Speers
	Brad Tippett
1984	Jim McCauley
1985	Mark Chiamp
1986	Jeff Norton
1987	Brad Jones
1988	Warren Sharples
1989	Todd Brost
1990	Warren Sharples
1991	Denny Felsner
1992	Denny Felsner
1993	Steve Shields
1994	Brian Wiseman
1995	Mike Knuble
1996	Brendan Morrison
1997	Brendan Morrison
1998	Marty Turco
1999	Josh Blackburn
2000	Mike Comrie
2001	Josh Blackburn
2002	Josh Blackburn,
	Mike Cammalleri
	Jed Ortmeyer
2003	Jed Ortmeyer
2004	Al Montoya
2005	T.J. Hensick
	Jeff Tambellini
2006	Andrew Ebbett
2007	T.J. Hensick
2008	Kevin Porter
2009	Louie Caporusso
2010	Carl Hagelin

Vic Heyliger Trophy—Outstanding Defenseman

Presented to the most valuable defenseman, as chosen by the members of the team. This trophy honors the former player and coach who led his Michigan teams to six NCAA championships in his 13 years of coaching.

1979	Tim Manning	1987	Jeff Norton	1995	Steven Halko	2003	Andy Burnes
1980	Tim Manning	1988	Myles O'Connor	1996	Steven Halko	2004	Brandon Rogers
1981	Tim Manning	1989	Myles O'Connor	1997	Harold Schock	2005	Matt Hunwick
1982	Dave Richter	1990	Alex Roberts	1998	Bubba Berenzweig	2006	Matt Hunwick
1983	Mike Neff	1991	Pat Neaton	1999	Bubba Berenzweig	2007	Matt Hunwick
1984	Todd Carlile	1992	David Harlock	2000	Jeff Jillson	2008	Mark Mitera
1985	Jeff Norton	1993	David Harlock	2001	Jeff Jillson	2009	Chris Summers
1986	Jeff Norton	1994	Steven Halko	2002	Andy Burnes	2010	Steve Kampfer

Penalties—Season

60	Chris Tamer	1989–90
58	Chris Tamer	1991–92
56	Cam Stewart	1990–91
55	Alex Roberts	1986–87
54	Jack Johnson	2005–06
54	Alex Roberts	1988–89
54	Aaron Ward	1990–91
53	Ross Morrison	1961–62
53	Dean Turner	1976–77
52	Doug Lindskog	1975–76
52	Chris Tamer	1990–91
51	Jason Botterill	1994–95
51	Myles O'Connor	1986–87
49	Cam Stewart	1991–92
48	Chris Tamer	1992–93

Penalties—Career

218	Chris Tamer	1990–93
191	Alex Roberts	1987–90
169	Jason Botterill	1994–97
169	Warren Luhning	1994–97
159	Myles O'Connor	1986–89
135	Cam Stewart	1991–93
133	Todd Copeland	1987–90
132	Todd Carlile	1983–86
130	Jeff Norton	1985–87
129	Ted Kramer	1989–92
127	Greg Fox	1973–76
126	Brian Lundberg	1979–82
124	Matt Hunwick	2004–07
120	John Blum	1978–81
120	Harold Schock	1994–97

Penalty Minutes—Season

149	Jack Johnson	2005–06
147	Chris Tamer	1989–90
143	Jason Botterill	1995–96
137	Doug Lindskog	1975–76
130	Chris Tamer	1990–91
129	Jason Botterill	1996–97
126	Aaron Ward	1990–91
125	Chris Tamer	1991–92
123	Warren Luhning	1995–96
120	Ross Morrison	1961–62
117	Jason Botterill	1994–95
117	Alex Roberts	1986–87
116	Alex Roberts	1988–89
115	Jeff Jillson	1999–2000
114	Bobby Hayes	1998–99

Penalty Minutes—Career

515	Chris Tamer	1990–93
483	Jason Botterill	1994–97
415	Alex Roberts	1987–90
392	Warren Luhning	1994–97
353	Myles O'Connor	1986–89
311	Greg Fox	1973–76
297	Cam Stewart	1991–93
296	Ted Kramer	1989–92
283	Jeff Norton	1985–87
283	Todd Carlile	1983–86
280	Bobby Hayes	1996–99
279	Todd Copeland	1987–90
277	Dale Rominski	1996–99
271	Brian Lundberg	1979–82
268	Sean Peach	1997–2000

CCHA Player of the Year

1994 David Oliver
1996 Brendan Morrison
1997 Brendan Morrison
2008 Kevin Porter

CCHA Coach of the Year

1994 Red Berenson
2008 Red Berenson

CCHA Rookie of the Year

1982 Jon Elliott
1983 Chris Seychel
1990 David Roberts
1991 Brian Wiseman
1994 Brendan Morrison
1995 Marty Turco
1999 Mike Comrie
2003 Jeff Tambellini
2004 T.J. Hensick
2008 Max Pacioretty
2009 David Wohlberg

CCHA Best Defensive Forward

1994 Mike Stone
1997 John Madden
2003 Jed Ortmeyer
2004 Dwight Helminen
2005 Eric Nystrom
2009 Tim Miller

CCHA Best Offensive Defenseman

2000 Jeff Jillson
2007 Jack Johnson

CCHA Best Defensive Defenseman

1995 Steven Halko
2002 Mike Komisarek
2007 Matt Hunwick

CCHA Terry Flanagan Memorial Award

2000 Sean Peach

CCHA Ilitch Humanitarian Award

2002 Kevin O'Malley
2007 Tim Cook

All-CCHA First Team

1983	Ted Speers
1987	Brad Jones
1989	Myles O'Connor
1991	Denny Felsner
1992	Denny Felsner
1993	Pat Neaton, Steve Shields
1994	David Oliver, Steve Shields, Brian Wiseman
1995	Brendan Morrison
1996	Kevin Hilton, Brendan Morrison
1997	John Madden, Brendan Morrison, Marty Turco
1998	Bill Muckalt
2000	Mike Comrie, Jeff Jillson
2001	Mike Cammalleri, Andy Hilbert, Jeff Jillson
2002	Mike Komisarek
2004	T.J. Hensick
2005	T.J. Hensick, Jeff Tambellini
2007	T.J. Hensick, Matt Hunwick, Jack Johnson
2008	Kevin Porter, Chad Kolarik
2009	Louie Caporusso, Aaron Palushaj

All-CCHA Second Team

1982	Jon Elliott, Steve Richmond
1986	Brad Jones
1987	Jeff Norton
1989	Todd Brost
1991	Pat Neaton, David Roberts
1993	David Oliver, David Roberts
1994	Mike Knuble
1995	Steven Halko, Mike Knuble
1996	Jason Botterill, Steven Halko
1997	Harold Schock
1998	Bubba Berenzweig, Bobby Hayes, Marty Turco
2000	Dave Huntzicker
2001	Josh Blackburn
2002	Mike Cammalleri, John Shouneyia
2003	Jeff Tambellini
2004	Al Montoya, Brandon Rogers
2005	Matt Hunwick
2006	T.J. Hensick, Matt Hunwick
2007	Kevin Porter
2008	Mark Mitera

All-CCHA Honorable Mention

1982	Ted Speers
1983	Brad Tippett
1984	Mark Chiamp
1986	Jeff Norton
1987	Myles O'Connor
1990	Denny Felsner, Warren Sharples
1992	Pat Neaton, David Oliver, Chris Tamer, Aaron Ward
1994	Steven Halko
1995	Kevin Hilton, Blake Sloan, Marty Turco
1996	John Madden, Blake Sloan
1999	Mike Van Ryn
2002	Josh Blackburn
2003	Al Montoya
2005	Eric Nystrom, Brandon Rogers
2007	Andrew Cogliano
2008	Billy Sauer
2009	Chad Langlais, Chris Summers

CCHA All-Rookie Team

1989	Denny Felsner
1990	Pat Neaton, David Roberts
1991	David Oliver, Aaron Ward, Brian Wiseman
1994	Jason Botterill, Brendan Morrison, Harold Schock, Blake Sloan
1995	Robb Gordon, Bill Muckalt, Marty Turco
1998	Mark Kosick, Mike Van Ryn
1999	Josh Blackburn, Mike Comrie, Jeff Jillson
2000	Andy Hilbert
2001	Mike Komisarek
2002	Eric Nystrom, Eric Werner
2003	Al Montoya, Danny Richmond, Jeff Tambellini
2004	T.J. Hensick, Matt Hunwick
2006	Andrew Cogliano, Jack Johnson
2008	Max Pacioretty
2009	Brandon Burlon, David Wohlberg
2010	Chris Brown

CCHA All-Tournament Team

1990	Mark Ouimet
1991	Don Stone, Aaron Ward
1992	Pat Neaton, Brian Wiseman
1994	Steven Halko, Blake Sloan, Mike Stone, Brian Wiseman
1996	Bobby Hayes, John Madden, Harold Schock
1997	Jason Botterill, Brendan Morrison
1999	Josh Blackburn, Mark Kosick, Sean Ritchlin, Mike Van Ryn
2001	Dave Huntzicker, Joe Kautz
2002	Josh Blackburn, Mike Cammalleri, Mike Komisarek, Jed Ortmeyer
2003	Dwight Helminen, Al Montoya, Jed Ortmeyer, Brandon Rogers
2004	Brandon Kaleniecki
2005	Brandon Rogers, Jeff Tambellini
2006	Matt Hunwick
2007	T.J. Hensick, Jack Johnson, Kevin Porter
2008	Tim Miller, Mark Mitera
2009	Louie Caporusso, Steve Kampfer
2010	Shawn Hunwick, Steve Kampfer, Louie Caporusso, Carl Hagelin

Bill Beagan Award—CCHA Tournament MVP

1994	Mike Stone
1996	John Madden
1997	Brendan Morrison
1999	Mark Kosick
2002	Mike Cammalleri
2003	Jed Ortmeyer
2005	Jeff Tambellini
2008	Tim Miller
2010	Shawn Hunwick

AHCA Spencer Penrose Award—Division I National Coach of the Year

1954 Vic Heyliger
2008 Red Berenson

AHCA Terry Flanagan Award—Assistant Coach's Career Body of Work

2000 Mel Pearson
2006 Billy Powers

Humanitarian Award

1997 Blake Sloan

The Hockey News—U.S. College Player of the Year

1994 David Oliver
1996 Brendan Morrison
1997 Brendan Morrison

NCAA Most Outstanding Player

1953 John Matchefts
1956 Lorne Howes
1964 Bob Gray
1996 Brendan Morrison
1998 Marty Turco

NCAA Regional Most Outstanding Player

1995 West Mike Knuble
1996 West Bill Muckalt
1997 West Jason Botterill
2001 West Mike Cammalleri
2003 Midwest Al Montoya
2008 East Kevin Porter

NCAA All-Tournament First Team

1948	Connie Hill, Wally Grant
1949	Wally Grant
1950	Ross Smith
1951	Bob Heathcott, Gil Burford, Neil Celley, John Matchefts
1952	Jim Haas, George Chin, John McKennell, Doug Philpott
1953	Alex MacLellan, John Matchefts
1955	Lorne Howes, Bill MacFarland, Tom Rendall
1956	Lorne Howes, Bob Pitts, Bob Schiller, Tom Rendall, Ed Switzer
1957	Bob Pitts, Tom Rendall
1962	Red Berenson
1964	Bob Gray, Tom Polonic, Gordon Wilkie
1977	Dave Debol
1996	Marty Turco, Steven Halko, Brendan Morrison
1998	Marty Turco, Bubba Berenzweig, Mark Kosick, Josh Langfeld

NCAA All-Tournament Second Team

1948	Wally Gacek, Ross Smith
1949	Wally Gacek, Connie Hill
1950	Wally Grant
1951	Hal Downes
1952	Reggie Shave, Earl Keyes
1953	Willard Ikola, Reggie Shave, George Chin
1954	Jim Haas, Bill MacFarland
1955	Bob Schiller, Mike Buchanan, Dick Dunnigan
1957	Ross Childs, Bob Schiller, Dick Dunnigan
1962	Larry Babcock, Don Rodgers
1964	Jack Cole, Barry MacDonald, Mel Wakabayashi

NCAA All-Regional Team

1994 West	Mike Stone
1995 West	Mike Knuble
1996 West	Brendan Morrison, Bill Muckalt
1997 West	Blake Sloan, Brendan Morrison, Jason Botterill
1998 West	Mike Van Ryn, Matt Herr, Mark Kosick
1999 East	Josh Blackburn, Bubba Berenzweig
2000 East	Mike Comrie
2001 West	Mike Cammalleri
2002 West	Josh Blackburn, Mike Komisarek, Jed Ortmeyer
2003 Midwest	Andy Burnes, Al Montoya, Eric Nystrom, Jed Ortmeyer
2004 Northeast	Al Montoya, Andy Burnes, Brandon Kaleniecki
2005 Midwest	Al Montoya, Brandon Rogers, Jeff Tambellini
2008 East	Kevin Porter, Chad Kolarik, Mark Mitera, Billy Sauer
2010 Midwest	Carl Hagelin

Photo Credits

Bentley Historical Library (University of Michigan) for photos on pages 2, 6, 10, 12, 24, 34, 36, 40, 42, 48, 52, 56, 62, 68, 78, and 80.

Mark Hicks, WestSide Photographic, LLC (Novi, MI), for photos on pages 18, 22, 28, 39, 44, 50, 61, 64, 66, 70, 82, 87, and 111.

Adam Jacobs, Adam Jacobs Photography (Ann Arbor, MI) for the cover photo and photos on pages 4 and 46.

Michigan Photo Services for the photo on page 74.

Wolverine Photo for photos on pages 1, 8, 14, 17, 20, 30, 32, 54, 58, and 72.

Thanks to Greg Kinney, Scott Galvin, Amir Gamzu, and Matt Trevor for their help.